Sweet UTOPIA

SIMPLY STUNNING VEGAN DESSERTS

Sharon Valencik

with photos by MILAN VALENCIK

D1557907

BOOK PUBLISHING COMPANY
Summertown, Tennessee

Library of Congress Cataloging-in-Publication Data

Valencik, Sharon.
   Sweet utopia : simply stunning vegan desserts / by Sharon Valencik ; with photography by Milan Valencik.
      p.   cm.
   Includes index.
   ISBN 978-1-57067-233-0
1. Desserts.   2. Vegan cookery.   I. Title.
   TX773.V324 2009
   641.8'6—dc22

2009026215

Food stylist: *Milan Valencik*
Cover and interior design: *Aerocraft Charter Art Service*

Printed in Hong Kong

Book Publishing Company
P.O. Box 99
Summertown, TN 38483
888-260-8458
www.bookpubco.com

ISBN-13 978-1-57067-233-0

17 16 15 14 13 12 11 10 09   1 2 3 4 5 6 7 8 9

Book Publishing Co. is a member of Green Press Initiative. We chose to print this title on paper with postconsumer recycled content, processed without chlorine, which saved the following natural resources:

89 trees
2,464 pounds of solid waste
40,577 gallons of wastewater
8,425 pounds of greenhouse gases
28 million BTU of total energy

For more information, visit www.greenpressinitiative.org.

Paper calculations from Environmental Defense Paper Calculator, www.papercalculator.org

Seize the moment.
Remember all those women on the Titanic
who waved off the dessert cart.

ERMA BOMBECK

Yield to temptation.
It may not pass your way again.

ROBERT HEINLEIN, *TIME ENOUGH FOR LOVE*

lemon love cups, page 153

Contents

Brown sugar, applesauce, spices, flour.
Put it in the oven for half an hour.

SPRINGTIME FOR MAX & RUBY

chocolate sausage, page 142

Preface

Welcome to *Sweet Utopia*, your source for scrumptious, simple, and sophisticated dessert recipes completely free of dairy products and eggs. Here you will find a wide array of goodies that you can create and enjoy whether you are vegan, are allergic to dairy and/or eggs, are watching your cholesterol and intake of saturated fat, or just love to make sweets. You can even find many recipes without nuts, too. There is no compromising on flavor or texture here—just delicious desserts for everyone to enjoy.

I come from a lineage of creative chef matriarchs who taught me that food is an art and a creative process. We don't settle for bland food; we strive to create something exciting to the taste buds. I chose to become vegan many years ago, but I simply was not willing to give up the joy of eating delicious desserts. So for me, my dietary restrictions were not about being restricted: they were a creative challenge.

I am a vegan connoisseur who has traveled to most of the vegan restaurants in the country, and I'm always on the lookout for more, domestically and around the world. For years I have enjoyed tempting both omnivores and vegans with my scrumptious vegan creations. Friends always ask me for advice on health, nutrition, and cooking uniquely wonderful treats. Sharing my experience and the simplicity of good vegan cooking is very fulfilling for me.

I am also a working mom of two young sons, so I know what a harried lifestyle is, and I know that complicated dessert recipes are simply not an option most of the time. Whenever the mood strikes, I take a few minutes to make one of my desserts because they are so simple, quick, and vital to the happiness of my family. Life just requires special treats at times!

It can seem intimidating to be vegan if you are a connoisseur of fine food, but the good news is that it is getting easier every day. I love the timeless, traditional sweets and family favorites that have been passed down to me from my mom and from her mom, and I have dedicated myself to transforming them into vegan versions that still manage to capture the flavors and textures of the originals. I share my secrets with you here in *Sweet Utopia*. These easy-to-make yet sensational recipes will entice you to rethink your notion of alternative desserts made without animal products. Prepare to indulge!

vanilla-agave crème brûlée, page 128

Introduction

Glistening chocolate hugging the edges of a rich cake, brilliant berries arranged meticulously over multiple tiers, a bright lemon loaf dotted with poppy seeds, begging to be bitten. Would you ever guess these were vegan?

Yes, you can absolutely still experience all the timeless, traditional sweets you love! The key to creating these desserts is using a few vegan staples for baking. These products are stocked at most supermarkets, gourmet and specialty shops, and virtually all natural food stores. With these ingredients, delicious flavors can be produced with ease.

Vegan food has transcended its niche and is now popular among those aware of its health properties and lower environmental impact. Allergies to dairy foods are skyrocketing, and vegan choices are the perfect solution for such sensitivities. Many people do not eat animal products for religious or spiritual reasons, so vegan options have also become popular among those who keep kosher or who do not mix meat and dairy products at a meal.

There is a growing demand for healthful cuisine as current research has raised public awareness of the dangers of consuming animal products and saturated fats. Even the USDA includes an impressive variety of vegan selections in every category of its latest food pyramid. Vegan diets are viewed more favorably than ever before, and the commercial options now available are expansive.

"Green" is the buzzword of the new century, due to a revived global consciousness and a renewed sense of caring about the earth. We are becoming more aware of where our food comes from and how it is produced.

pumpkin cheesecake pie, page 98

Using plant-based ingredients is a great way to reduce environmental degradation, because using land to raise food for human consumption, rather than for grazing farmed animals or growing the crops to feed them, is less intensive, more resource efficient, and, when produced organically, more earth friendly.

There is also a vibrant trend toward purchasing locally grown, seasonal produce from sustainable farms. Buying locally reduces the carbon dioxide emissions caused by transporting food long distances—from other states, countries, or continents—and it boosts the local economy as well. Plus, local foods tend to be more diverse, fresher, and tastier.

There is no better time than right now to begin using vegan alternatives for all your dietary needs. Let's get started by making vegan desserts you can feel great about!

strawberry fields cake with
unbeetable buttercream frosting, page 37

Stocking
THE KITCHEN

Having the right equipment and necessary ingredients on hand will allow you to make all of the delicious recipes in this book right when you crave them, without running out to the store. The recipes are designed to be flexible, so you can mix and match ingredients as you like. The more staple items you have in your pantry, the more easily you'll be able to substitute the ingredients you most prefer.

basic supplies and tools

choco-choco sandwich minis, page 80

- aluminum foil
- baking pan, rectangular (9 x 13 inch)
- baking pan, square (8 inch and 9 inch)
- baking sheets (preferably insulated)
- box grater
- cake pans, round (8 inch)
- colander
- cookie cutters (a variety of shapes and sizes)
- jelly-roll pan (13 x 18 inch)
- loaf pan (9 inch)
- muffin pan liners, mini and standard (foil and/or paper)

*chocolate-cherry candy cups,
page 143*

- muffin pans, mini and standard
- nonstick pan liners, such as Silpat (various sizes)
- parchment paper
- peeler
- pie pan (9 inch)
- pizza cutter (rolling)
- plastic wrap
- rolling pin
- saucepans (small, medium, and large)
- sifter (fine)
- spatulas (rubber and metal)
- springform pan (9 inch)
- steamer
- toothpicks
- waxed paper
- whisk
- wooden spoons
- zester or Microplane grater

electric equipment

Blender. Purchase the largest, highest-quality, and most powerful blender you can afford. A blender is indispensable for producing extra-creamy, perfectly smooth textures. This is especially important when processing tofu and soy cream cheese mixtures. Due to the limited capacity of most standard blenders, mixtures will often need to be processed in batches.

Food processor. Consider your food processor an investment and get the best model you can afford. A high-quality food processor is essential for creating smooth and creamy cheesecakes, crèmes, and mousses, as well as for grinding nuts and processing graham crackers and bread into fine crumbs.

Grinder. An electric coffee grinder or spice mill is an inexpensive gadget that is great for powdering granulated sugar and grinding flaxseeds, rolled oats, nuts, and spices. Have one that is used only for baking purposes and another for grinding coffee beans, so the flavor of coffee isn't unintentionally transferred to your desserts.

Mixer. Use either an electric hand mixer or a stand mixer for creaming vegan margarine and sugar or whipping up a batter. Avoid using a mixer for processing tofu and soy cream cheese, as it will not get them completely smooth.

ingredients

EXTRACTS, SPICES, AND FLAVORINGS

blueberry-lemon scones, page 158

- almond extract
- anise extract
- cardamom, ground
- cinnamon, ground
- cloves, ground
- cocoa powder, unsweetened (regular and Dutch)
- coconut extract
- ginger, candied or crystallized
- ginger, ground
- green tea powder
- lemon extract
- liqueur (amaretto, cherry, chocolate, coffee, hazelnut, orange)
- nutmeg, ground
- orange extract
- orange peel, candied
- peppermint extract
- spirits (rum, whiskey, and others)
- turmeric, ground
- vanilla beans, whole
- vanilla extract

FRESH PRODUCE

- apples
- bananas
- carrots
- lemons
- limes
- oranges
- spinach
- tangerines
- zucchini

coconut heaven cake with coconut buttercream frosting, page 29

FROZEN FOODS

- berries (blueberries, mixed berries, raspberries, strawberries)
- mango chunks
- phyllo dough
- puff pastry
- soy ice cream (vanilla and other favorite flavors)
- spinach

layered cream gels with fruit, page 125

REFRIGERATED FOODS

- almond butter, unsalted creamy
- almonds, raw (sliced, slivered, and whole)
- cashew butter, unsalted
- cashews, raw
- chocolate syrup
- hazelnuts, raw
- margarine, vegan (preferably Earth Balance brand)
- nondairy milk (almond, hemp, oat, nut, rice, soy)
- nutmeg, whole
- peanut butter, crunchy and creamy
- pecans, raw
- pignolia nuts, raw
- soy cream cheese, plain
- soy creamer (plain and vanilla)

- soy whipped cream
- tofu, regular and extra-firm
- walnuts, raw

PANTRY STAPLES

- agar powder
- agave syrup
- applesauce, unsweetened
- apricot halves, canned
- baking powder, aluminum free (preferably Rumford brand)
- baking soda
- canola oil, liquid and spray
- chickpea flour
- chocolate bars, nondairy
- chocolate chips, nondairy (many store brands are vegan)
- coconut cream, sweetened
- coconut milk, full-fat
- coconut oil
- coconut, dried shredded (sweetened or unsweetened)
- corn syrup (preferably organic)
- cornstarch (preferably organic)
- dates (whole or chopped)
- flaxseeds (whole or meal)
- fruit, dried (apricots, cherries, cranberries, pineapple, raisins)
- graham cracker pie crust (most brands are vegan)
- graham crackers (vegan)
- maple syrup
- molasses, blackstrap (preferably organic)
- nondairy milk, in aseptic cartons (plain or vanilla)
- olive oil, light
- peaches, canned
- pineapple, canned (chunks, crushed, and rings)
- pumpkin, canned

lemon-berry tart, page 108

sesame cookies, page 61

- quick-cooking tapioca
- rolled oats, old-fashioned
- rolled oats, quick-cooking
- sandwich cookies (vegan)
- sea salt
- sesame seeds, raw
- sesame seeds, toasted
- spelt flour
- sugar, brown (preferably organic)
- sugar, granulated (preferably organic turbinado)
- sugar, powdered (preferably organic)
- tea biscuits (vegan; see sidebar below)
- tofu, silken (firm and soft)
- unbleached all-purpose flour
- vinegar, apple cider
- vinegar, white distilled
- wafer cookies (vegan)
- wheat germ
- whole wheat flour
- whole wheat pastry flour

TEA BISCUITS

Tea biscuits are more delicate than graham crackers and most other cookies. They are the vegan version of *petit beurre,* the French butter biscuits that contain milk. Look for them in the kosher section of your supermarket and in specialty stores, or explore online outlets for dairy-free tea biscuits in plain, vanilla, chocolate, or other flavors. You can substitute digestive biscuits, graham crackers, or another type of cookie if you have trouble finding tea biscuits.

Succeed
IN VEGAN BAKING

Tips for Creating Luscious Vegan Desserts

ingredient tips

LIKE BUTTA

I learned the hard way that you can't bake with plain old margarine instead of a high-quality, great-tasting, spreadable, nonhydrogenated, vegan butter alternative like Earth Balance brand. Earth Balance lends a rich, buttery flavor to cookies and has just the right consistency. It comes in sticks and tubs, and either is fine to use. You can find it in well-stocked supermarkets, specialty gourmet shops, and natural food stores. Because it is salted, I try to limit added salt in my recipes that call for this product. There are other vegan butter substitutes available, but in my experience, Earth Balance is far superior for baking.

Vegan butter substitutes must be at room temperature or softened prior to using them for baking. This can be achieved by letting the uncovered container rest on the countertop for 30 minutes. If you don't have time to leave the container out of the refrigerator for this amount of time, you can pop it in the microwave for 10 seconds to soften the spread a bit; this will make it easier for you to cream it with the sugar. Take care, however, as vegan butter substitutes melt very quickly. When you need it slightly softened but not quite at room temperature, let it sit for about 10 minutes. Don't leave it out for too long or it will become too soft to work with and will make your desserts mushy.

apple strudel, page 168

NONDAIRY CHOCOLATE

Natural food stores generally stock nondairy chocolate chips and chocolate bars for cooking and baking, and often they are organic. If you are shopping at a mainstream supermarket, read the ingredient list on the product package to ensure there is no milk powder or whey in the chocolate. An exciting new product is rice milk chocolate, a creamy, light, multipurpose chocolate that is great to use for dipping candy balls.

You can melt chocolate several ways: in a bowl or double boiler over barely simmering water; in a glass or ceramic bowl in a pot of shallow, barely simmering water; or in a glass or ceramic bowl in the microwave. To melt chocolate in the microwave, use medium power. Microwave for 1 minute, then remove the bowl and stir. If necessary, place the bowl back in the microwave and heat again for 25 seconds. Repeat if needed. Whichever method you choose, make sure you stir the chocolate frequently to help it melt more evenly. After it is fully melted, stir it until smooth. Take care that the chocolate doesn't burn.

simplest rich chocolate cake with chocolate frosting, page 22

SOY CREAM CHEESE

Soy-based nondairy cream cheese (sometimes called tofu cream cheese) is sold at most well-stocked supermarkets and natural food stores. When used in baking, it adds a rich taste similar to sour cream and also makes for flaky dough and creamy fillings. Do not freeze soy cream cheese or the texture will be altered. Many containers of soy cream cheese contain one cup (eight ounces).

EGG ALTERNATIVES

My recipes do not require egg substitutes. If you are converting a conventional recipe and need a replacement for eggs, here are some mixtures you can try. Each of the options that follow will replace one egg.

For Binding or Moistening

- 2 to 3 tablespoons of applesauce or puréed fruit
- ½ large banana, mashed
- 1 tablespoon of finely ground flaxseeds mixed with 2 tablespoons of water
- 3 tablespoons of silken tofu blended with 1 tablespoon of water
- 2 tablespoons of flour or starch (cornstarch, potato starch, or arrowroot) mixed with 1 tablespoon of water

For Leavening

- Ener-G Egg Replacer powder (follow the package directions)
- ½ teaspoon of baking soda mixed with 1 teaspoon of white vinegar

FLOUR

I created my recipes so you could make the most delicious vegan treats ever, not necessarily the most healthful ones. When I use the term "all-purpose flour," I am referring to unbleached white flour. This flour yields the best-tasting results for each recipe. However, if you want to use part whole wheat pastry flour, white whole wheat flour, all-purpose whole wheat flour, or spelt flour, go right ahead; feel free to experiment.

Whole wheat flour contains the entire wheat kernel (bran, germ, and endosperm); white flour has the bran and germ removed, so only the starchy endosperm remains. Whole wheat pastry flour is made from a strain of wheat that is lower in gluten than whole wheat bread flour or whole wheat all-purpose flour. It is a good flour to try in your baking. Begin by replacing half of the regular flour in a recipe with whole wheat pastry flour. It might alter the flavor a bit and make the cake or cookie more dense. See how it suits your taste and try substituting more or less next time. Whole wheat bread flour is not recommended for use in baked desserts.

White whole wheat flour is made from a new strain of albino wheat; it is a whole-grain flour that is sweeter and milder than the slightly bitter red wheat used for whole wheat flour. It is a great replacement for white flour and will yield similar results.

zucchini loaf cake with a tangerine twist, page 33

DRIED FRUIT AND COCONUT

Look for unsulfured dried fruits in your natural food store. If you are really ambitious, you can use a dehydrator to make your own dried fruits. Although sweetened dried coconut tastes best in recipes, it usually contains preservatives. If you use unsweetened dried coconut in cookies, you may need to increase the amount of sugar slightly.

NUTMEG

I keep whole nutmeg in the refrigerator or freezer in a heavy-duty zipper-lock bag. This way I am able to grate it finely for fresh, bold flavor. Ground nutmeg also works well in all the recipes in the book. Measurements for grated or ground nutmeg are the same.

GOT SOYMILK?

Although I call for soymilk in my recipes, feel free to use any nondairy milk you prefer. Plain or vanilla flavors can be used unless a particular flavor is specified. All of the recipes use sweetened soymilk unless otherwise stated. If you are using unsweetened nondairy milk, you will need to add more sweetener to the recipe.

Don't have any nondairy milk on hand? It's easy to make your own. Simply soak ½ cup of raw nuts (such as cashews or almonds) for 2 to 4 hours in water to cover; then drain and rinse. Alternatively, use ½ cup of sesame seeds or tahini. Process them in a blender with 2 cups of water until smooth and strain through cheesecloth or a fine-mesh strainer.

HOW SWEET IT IS

Most sugar is not produced sustainably, and many brands of cane sugar are not vegan (they are filtered through animal bone char). Commercial brown sugar is simply refined white sugar with molasses added to it. Fortunately, it is now easy to find a variety of organic, fair-trade sugar products in various crystal sizes and colors in natural food stores, gourmet shops, and many well-stocked supermarkets. Vegan sugars may be labeled as demerara sugar, evaporated cane juice, natural sugar, organic sugar, raw sugar, turbinado sugar, and unbleached sugar. Unless turbinado, brown, or powdered sugar is specified in a recipe, use the lightest-colored vegan sugar available. Turbinado and raw sugar may be used interchangeably in the recipes.

WORKING WITH VINEGAR

almond cheesecake, page 99

Vinegar is truly an amazing product for vegan baking, natural cleaning, and natural health purposes. Vinegar, which is chemically acetic, reacts with the baking soda (sodium bicarbonate) in a recipe to add bubbles, causing a cake to rise. It is important to gently fold a mixture that contains vinegar—do not beat it—or you will put a damper on the chemical reaction. White vinegar is milder than cider vinegar, but either can be used. Unless I am preparing a fruity cake, I usually prefer distilled white vinegar for baking because it doesn't impart any flavor.

WHERE DO I FIND IT?

The ingredients used in this book can be found at natural food stores and most well-stocked supermarkets. Asian markets are a great resource for a number of items you'll need to make the recipes in this book, such as coconut cream, coconut milk, green tea powder, sesame seeds, and regular and silken tofu. Ingredients that you cannot track down locally can be purchased from online retailers.

ZESTY

I refer to lemon and orange zest as "finely grated peel." They mean the same thing. To obtain the peel, or zest, use a zester (a tool designed specifically for this purpose), a very fine grater, or a Microplane grater and gently take off only the colored part of the peel. Don't use the white pith, as it is bitter.

procedural tips

COOL IT

You don't need to run out and buy metal cooling racks if you don't already have them. Delicate cookies and cutouts should be cooled on their baking sheets for a few minutes to keep them from breaking (using insulated baking sheets, nonstick pan liners, or parchment paper will help keep them from sticking and make them easier to remove). Once the cookies are removed from their baking sheets, place them on a flat surface or dish lined with parchment paper until they are completely cool and ready to be transferred to cookie tins or plastic containers for storage.

GET READY

Make sure that you have all of your measuring cups, spoons, whisks, and other equipment handy, clean, and ready to use before you get started on a recipe. Do any prep work, such as chopping nuts or grating nutmeg, prior to mixing the main ingredients.

HOW TO TOAST NUTS

Lightly toasting nuts really brings out their flavor and will make your desserts that much better. Cool the nuts completely before chopping or using them in a recipe.

To toast nuts on the stovetop, place them in a skillet on low to medium heat, stirring constantly with a wooden spoon so all sides of the nuts are evenly exposed to the heat. As soon as they turn a shade darker, transfer them to a glass or ceramic dish to cool.

To toast nuts in the oven, preheat the oven to 350 degrees F and spread the nuts in a single layer on a baking sheet. Stir the nuts every few minutes, watching closely so they don't become too dark, and spread them out again into a single layer. After 6 to 8 minutes, the nuts will be toasted. Transfer them immediately to a glass or ceramic dish to cool.

Substitutions, Equivalents, and Conversions

What if I don't have some of these ingredients?

This book is meant to include everyone—vegans, vegetarians, aspiring vegans, and nonvegans alike. If you don't have access to some of the nondairy or organic ingredients, please don't worry about it. Most ingredients are easy to replace.

TABLE 1 ingredient alternatives

RECOMMENDED INGREDIENT	VEGAN ALTERNATIVES	NONVEGAN ALTERNATIVES
vegan butter substitute	Earth Balance spread or sticks are recommended for the best results, although other brands of vegan margarine may be used; if the spread you use contains salt, omit added salt in the recipe	unsalted butter
nondairy chocolate chips	■ carob chips (though they will alter the flavor) ■ chopped vegan chocolate bars (chopped by hand or pulsed in a food processor)	regular semisweet chocolate chips
organic granulated sugar	■ raw sugar ■ turbinado sugar	regular granulated sugar
organic powdered sugar	combine 2 cups granulated organic sugar with $\frac{1}{2}$ cup cornstarch in a food processor or coffee grinder and grind until finely powdered; store in an airtight container at room temperature	regular powdered sugar
organic brown sugar	add $\frac{1}{2}$ cup dark molasses (not blackstrap) to 1 cup organic granulated sugar and mix well; store in an airtight container at room temperature	regular brown sugar
soymilk	other nondairy milk (such as hemp milk, oat milk, nut milk, or rice milk), store-bought or homemade	cow's milk (preferably organic)
soy cream cheese	—	regular cream cheese
soy creamer	—	regular nondairy creamer or dairy cream

Can I use baking chocolate instead of chocolate chips?

For recipes that call for chocolate chips that are to be melted, you can substitute semisweet baking squares or bars.

TABLE 2 chocolate equivalents

CHOCOLATE CHIPS	SEMISWEET CHOCOLATE BAKING SQUARES
1 cup	6 ounces
¾ cup	4.5 ounces
⅔ cup	4 ounces
½ cup	3 ounces
⅓ cup	2 ounces
¼ cup	1½ ounces

pumpkin–chocolate chip muffins, page 49

What if I don't have the right type or size of pan?

You can use glass, ceramic, metal, or silicone pans, though I don't usually recommend silicone because the results may be unpredictable. If you use a larger pan than the recipe calls for, thereby making the depth of your batter more shallow, you will need to decrease the baking time by approximately one-quarter. Conversely, if you use a smaller pan and the depth of your batter increases, you will need to increase the baking time by about one-quarter.

TABLE 3 baking pan equivalents

RECIPE CALLS FOR	USE (inches)	(centimeters)
1 (9-inch) springform pan	2 (8-inch) round cake pans	2 (20-cm) round cake pans
	2 (9-inch) round cake pans	2 (23-cm) round cake pans
	1 (9-inch) square pan	1 (23-cm) square pan
	1 (10-inch) springform pan	1 (25-cm) springform pan
	1 (10-inch) round cake pan	1 (25-cm) round cake pan

(continued)

TABLE 3 baking pan equivalents (continued)

RECIPE CALLS FOR	USE (inches)	(centimeters)
1 (9-inch) loaf pan	1 (8-inch) square pan 1 (9-inch) square pan 1 (9-inch) round cake pan	1 (20-cm) square pan 1 (23-cm) square pan 1 (23-cm) round cake pan
2 (8-inch) round cake pans	2 (8-inch) loaf pans 2 (9-inch) round cake pans 2 (9-inch) round pie pans 1 (9-inch) tube pan 1 (9-inch) springform pan 1 (10-inch) springform pan 1 (10-inch) Bundt pan 1 (11-inch) round tart pan	2 (20-cm) loaf pans 2 (23-cm) round cake pans 2 (23-cm) round pie pans 1 (23-cm) tube pan 1 (23-cm) springform pan 1 (25-cm) springform pan 1 (25-cm) Bundt pan 1 (28-cm) round tart pan
1 (8-inch) square pan	1 (9-inch) pie pan 1 (9-inch) loaf pan 1 (7 x 11-inch) baking dish	1 (23-cm) pie pan 1 (23-cm) loaf pan 1 (17 x 28-cm) baking dish
1 (9-inch) pie pan	1 (9-inch) square pan 1 (9-inch) round pie pan 1 (9-inch) tart pan	1 (23-cm) square pan 1 (23-cm) round pie pan 1 (23-cm) tart pan
1 (9-inch) square pan	1 (9-inch) pie pan 1 (9-inch) round cake pan	1 (23-cm) pie pan 1 (23-cm) round cake pan
1 (9 x 13-inch) pan	2 (8-inch) round cake pans 2 (9-inch) round cake pans 1 (9-inch) tube pan 1 (10-inch) Bundt pan	2 (20-cm) round cake pans 2 (23-cm) round cake pans 2 (23-cm) tube pan 1 (25-cm) Bundt pan

coconut tiramisu, page 138

What if my oven always burns or undercooks cakes and cookies?

Ovens vary and baking times might need a slight adjustment from those listed in the book. Always preheat the oven and make sure your oven door closes tightly so the heat doesn't escape. Don't open the oven door when cakes and cookies are baking, and invest in an oven thermometer to make sure your oven heats to the correct temperature.

TABLE 4 temperature conversion chart

DEGREES F	DEGREES C
200	93
250	121
300	149
325	163
350	177
375	191

How can I convert U.S. measurements to metric?

TABLE 5 measurement conversions

CUP	FLUID OUNCES	TABLESPOONS	TEASPOONS	MILLILITERS
1 cup	8 ounces	16 tablespoons	48 teaspoons	237 milliliters
³/₄ cup	6 ounces	12 tablespoons	36 teaspoons	177 milliliters
²/₃ cup	5 ¹/₃ ounces	10.6 tablespoons	32 tablespoons	158 milliliters
¹/₂ cup	4 ounces	8 tablespoons	24 teaspoons	118 milliliters
¹/₃ cup	2 ²/₃ ounces	5.3 tablespoons	16 teaspoons	79 milliliters
¹/₄ cup	2 ounces	4 tablespoons	12 teaspoons	59 milliliters
¹/₈ cup	1 ounce	2 tablespoons	6 teaspoons	30 milliliters
¹/₁₆ cup	¹/₂ ounce	1 tablespoon	3 teaspoons	15 milliliters

sticky toffee pudding, page 44

TABLE 6 math conversion table

MULTIPLY	BY	TO GET
inches	25.4	millimeters
ounces	28.35	grams
pounds	.45359	kilograms

Decadent
CAKES

Dost thou think, because thou art virtuous,
there shall be no more cakes and ale?

WILLIAM SHAKESPEARE, *TWELFTH NIGHT*

Are you looking for cakes with a twist, or do you want something simple? There are times you want to go for the unexpected and show off; other times you just want to mix up ingredients quickly and throw the pan in the oven. Whatever you're in the mood for, you'll find it in one of these rich and flavorful cakes.

You'll see that you don't need eggs to make moist, tender cakes that rise or dairy to make heavenly, creamy frostings and crème toppings. And you won't believe what you can bake up with no cholesterol whatsoever! Using straightforward ingredients, I've created a variety of the best cakes for entertaining; for when you just want a wholesome, homemade sweet treat in the house; or when you need something to send in a lunch bag. Learn how simple and easy it is to make vegan cakes. Indulge!

sweet utopia tips

BEAUTIFY

Decorating cakes is really fun and a great way to showcase your artistic talent. Try using fresh tropical fruit, frozen berries, edible glitter, or sprinkles. Store-bought frostings are often vegan (read the ingredient list), but they are not particularly healthful. On the upside, they are good for adding wording to cakes and doing fancy designs, plus they have a long shelf life and do not require refrigeration.

opposite: midnight cake with chocolate frosting, page 23

IS IT DONE YET?

You can tell that a cake is finished baking if the center bounces back when lightly pressed with a finger and a toothpick inserted into the center of the cake comes out clean.

EQUIP YOURSELF

These recipes use standard cake pans, but feel free to buy fancy versions and unusual shapes and sizes and try them out too.

EXPLORE

Look for decorating supplies at supermarkets and craft stores. I recommend buying an inexpensive pastry bag set so you can pipe frosting designs that will get lots of oohs and aahs. Even dollar stores can inspire creative design ideas. Take a stroll through your local stores and keep your eyes open for a myriad of decorating equipment.

FROSTING

Homemade vegan frostings are not like traditional frostings, since they are made with vegan butter substitute or soy cream cheese, which becomes soft

cocoa-berry cake with berry cream frosting, page 24

quickly and requires refrigeration. Thus I recommend that you either frost cakes no more than an hour before serving or refrigerate a frosted cake only up to a day in advance. If you've ever had a vegan cake with a long shelf life, the frosting was probably made with unsavory ingredients, such as a large quantity of sugar, artificial coloring, and hydrogenated shortening.

OIL IT

I like to "grease" baking pans and baking sheets the modern way, using organic vegetable oil spray. Vegetable oil spray makes this task simple and quick, with much less mess than using margarine. There is even a vegetable oil spray that has flour in it, allowing you to oil and flour a pan in one easy step. I prefer to use canola oil spray; look for brands that contain organic canola oil with natural propellants (no chlorofluorocarbons). If you prefer to use plain canola oil, apply a small amount to a clean cloth or pastry brush and spread a very thin film of it over the pan. To flour an oiled pan, sprinkle a little flour over it, shake and tap the pan to distribute the flour evenly over the bottom and sides, then shake off and discard the flour that doesn't stick.

*simplest rich chocolate cake
with chocolate frosting, page 22*

MIX IT UP

Be careful not to overmix your cake batter. Overmixing will reduce the delicate leavening properties of the vegan ingredients.

SHAPE IT

Many of the recipes in this section can be made into cupcakes. They can also be baked in other sizes and shapes of pans. See page 15 for information on substituting baking pans.

STORAGE

Most cakes, especially gooey and fruity ones, should be stored in the refrigerator for maximum freshness. Cakes should either be frosted right before they are served, or they can be frosted and put in the refrigerator, uncovered, for a few hours prior to serving. Leftovers should be covered and refrigerated. To cover them, use a cake storage container (also called a cake keeper), sealed plastic container, inverted bowl, plastic wrap, aluminum wrap, or any other covering of your choice. Unfrosted cakes may be covered loosely and stored at room temperature or in the refrigerator. Frostings should be kept refrigerated.

I love chocolate cake so much that I had to include two different recipes for it. This simple, rich, one-bowl cake delights everyone and also makes great cupcakes. It's a toned-down version of Midnight Cake (page 23), which is pure decadence.

simplest rich chocolate cake with chocolate frosting

*NUT FREE

CHOCOLATE CAKE

2½ cups all-purpose flour

1½ cups granulated sugar

½ cup unsweetened cocoa powder, sifted

2 teaspoons baking powder

½ teaspoon baking soda

½ teaspoon salt

2 cups soymilk

½ cup canola oil

1 teaspoon white vinegar

1 teaspoon vanilla extract

CHOCOLATE FROSTING

1½ cups nondairy chocolate chips

⅓ cup vegan butter substitute

½ cup powdered sugar, sifted

To make the cake, preheat the oven to 350 degrees F and oil and flour two 8-inch round cake pans. Combine the flour, sugar, cocoa, baking powder, baking soda, and salt in a large bowl. Add the soymilk, oil, vinegar, and vanilla extract and stir until just combined. Pour evenly into the prepared pans and bake for about 28 minutes, or until a toothpick inserted into the center comes out clean. Cool on racks.

To make the frosting, melt the chocolate chips and vegan butter substitute in a double boiler over gently simmering water. Alternatively, place them in a microwave-safe bowl and microwave at medium power for 1 minute. Stir. Microwave for 25 seconds longer and stir until smooth. If necessary, microwave for an additional 25 seconds. Stir in the powdered sugar and mix until smooth. Let the frosting cool for 8 to 10 minutes.

To assemble, remove the cooled cakes from the pans and spread about one-third of the frosting over 1 of the cakes. Place the other cake over it and frost the top and sides. Store uncovered in the refrigerator until serving time. Leftovers should be covered and stored in the refrigerator.

Note: For the best-tasting cake, use Dutch cocoa for at least half of the cocoa called for in the recipe. Dutch cocoa has been treated with an alkali to neutralize the cocoa's natural acidity, giving it a richer flavor and darker color.

Rich Chocolate Cupcakes: Oil and flour 18 standard muffin cups or use paper liners. Pour the cake batter evenly into the prepared cups and bake for 25 minutes, or until a toothpick inserted into the center comes out clean. Cool and frost. Makes 18 cupcakes.

This is a chocoholic's dream—decadent and romantic, perfect for a birthday or Valentine's Day. For the best-tasting cake, use Dutch cocoa for at least half of the cocoa called for in the recipe.

midnight cake with chocolate frosting

*NUT FREE   YIELD: 12 SERVINGS

MIDNIGHT CAKE

2 ⅓ cups all-purpose flour

¾ cup unsweetened cocoa powder

2 teaspoons baking powder

½ teaspoon baking soda

¼ teaspoon salt

⅔ cup vegan butter substitute, at room temperature

1 cup granulated sugar

½ cup powdered sugar

1 cup coconut milk

½ cup hot strong coffee

½ cup soymilk

2 teaspoons white vinegar

1 teaspoon vanilla extract

¾ teaspoon almond or additional vanilla extract

½ cup nondairy chocolate chips

½ cup shredded dried coconut (sweetened or unsweetened; optional)

CHOCOLATE FROSTING

1 ½ cups nondairy chocolate chips

⅓ cup vegan butter substitute

½ cup powdered sugar, sifted

To make the cake, preheat the oven to 350 degrees F and oil and flour two 8-inch round cake pans. Sift together the flour, cocoa, baking powder, baking soda, and salt into a bowl.

In a separate large bowl, combine the vegan butter substitute, granulated sugar, and powdered sugar and beat with a wooden spoon until smooth. Beat in the coconut milk, coffee, soymilk, vinegar, and extracts. Add the flour mixture and stir until just combined. Stir in the chocolate chips and optional coconut. Pour evenly into the prepared pans and bake for 25 to 28 minutes, or until a toothpick inserted into the center comes out clean. Cool on racks.

To make the frosting, melt the chocolate chips and vegan butter substitute in a double boiler over gently simmering water. Alternatively, place them in a microwave-safe bowl and microwave at medium power for 1 minute. Stir. Microwave for 25 seconds longer and stir until smooth. If necessary, microwave for an additional 25 seconds. Stir in the powdered sugar and mix until smooth. Let the frosting cool for 8 to 10 minutes.

To assemble, remove the cooled cakes from the pans and spread about one-third of the frosting over 1 of the cakes. Place the other cake over it and frost the top and sides. Serve shortly after assembling. Leftovers should be covered and stored in the refrigerator.

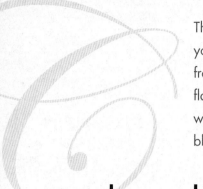

The berries "take the cake" in this recipe with their bold, antioxidant glow. If you want to show off your culinary talents, just make this colorful cake and frosting and your guests will be in awe. The cake has a light, pleasant cocoa flavor, and the batter makes great cupcakes. Kids love the color. Experiment with a variety of berries to produce different frosting hues: blueberries for blue, raspberries or strawberries for pink, or mixed berries for purple.

cocoa-berry cake with berry cream frosting

*NUT FREE   YIELD: 12 SERVINGS

COCOA-BERRY CAKE

½ cup fresh or thawed frozen berries (a single kind or a combination)

2 cups all-purpose flour

3 tablespoons unsweetened cocoa powder

2 teaspoons baking powder

½ teaspoon baking soda

1⅓ cups granulated sugar

½ cup vegan butter substitute, at room temperature

1 cup minus 2 tablespoons soymilk

2 teaspoons vanilla extract

1 teaspoon white vinegar

BERRY CREAM FROSTING

1¼ cup powdered sugar

½ cup soy cream cheese

⅓ cup vegan butter substitute, slightly softened but not at room temperature

1 teaspoon vanilla extract

To make the cake, preheat the oven to 350 degrees F and oil and flour two 8-inch round cake pans. Press the berries through a fine strainer or sieve to extract about 3 tablespoons of juice. Set the juice aside to put in the cake. Save the crushed berries to add to the frosting.

Combine the flour, cocoa, baking powder, and baking soda in a bowl and stir until there are no lumps. In a separate large bowl, combine the sugar and vegan butter substitute and beat with a wooden spoon until fluffy. Beat in the soymilk, reserved berry juice, vanilla extract, and vinegar. Add the flour mixture and stir until just combined. Pour evenly into the prepared pans and bake for about 28 minutes, or until a toothpick inserted into the center comes out clean. Cool on racks.

To make the frosting, combine the crushed berries, powdered sugar, soy cream cheese, vegan butter substitute, and vanilla extract in a food processor or blender and process until smooth and fluffy. Refrigerate the frosting while the cake is baking.

To assemble, remove the cooled cakes from the pans and spread about one-third of the frosting over 1 of the cakes. Place the other cake over it and frost the top and sides. Store uncovered in the refrigerator until serving time. Leftovers should be covered and stored in the refrigerator.

Variation: For a dramatic effect, replace the Berry Cream Frosting with Chocolate Frosting (page 23). Garnish the frosted cake with a variety of fresh berries.

Cocoa Berry Cupcakes: Oil and flour 14 standard muffin cups or use paper liners. Pour the cake batter evenly into the prepared cups and bake for 25 minutes, or until a toothpick inserted into the center comes out clean. Cool and frost. Makes 14 cupcakes.

Take a slice and hide the rest. Many years ago, my mother's traditional version of this cake was all the rage. I never thought I'd say it, but this version is even richer and tastier, especially if you love chocolate and nuts as I do. I've been told by many that it's the best cake they have ever tasted.

chocolate chip and nut streusel coffee cake

YIELD: 12 SERVINGS

COFFEE CAKE

2 cups all-purpose flour

2 teaspoons baking powder

½ teaspoon baking soda

¼ teaspoon salt

1¼ cups granulated sugar

1 cup soy cream cheese

½ cup vegan butter substitute, at room temperature

¾ cup soymilk

2 teaspoons white vinegar

1 teaspoon vanilla extract

1¼ cups nondairy chocolate chips

STREUSEL TOPPING

⅓ cup granulated, brown, or turbinado sugar

1½ teaspoons ground cinnamon

½ to ⅔ cup chopped walnuts or pecans

To make the cake, preheat the oven to 350 degrees F and oil and flour a 9-inch springform pan. Combine the flour, baking powder, baking soda, and salt in a bowl. In a separate large bowl, combine the sugar, soy cream cheese, and vegan butter substitute and beat with an electric mixer until smooth. Beat in the soymilk, vinegar, and vanilla extract. Add the flour mixture and stir with a wooden spoon until just combined. Fold in the chocolate chips. Pour half of the cake batter evenly into the prepared pan.

To make the streusel topping, combine the sugar and cinnamon. Add the nuts and toss until evenly mixed. Sprinkle half of the streusel topping over the batter in the pan. Pour the remaining batter evenly into the pan and sprinkle with the remaining streusel topping. Bake for 50 minutes, or until the cake is golden brown on top. Cool before removing from the pan and slicing.

Happy birthday! This sweet layer cake is perfect for a birthday party and intriguing enough to draw compliments when entertaining.

banana cake with banana caramel crème and roasted pecans

YIELD: 12 SERVINGS

BANANA CARAMEL CRÈME

½ large ripe banana, chopped

¾ cup brown sugar

¾ cup vanilla soy creamer, or ¾ plain soy creamer plus 2 tablespoons sugar and ½ teaspoon vanilla extract

2 tablespoons vegan butter substitute, at room temperature

¾ cup silken tofu, well drained

ROASTED PECANS

2 cups raw pecans

¼ cup vegan butter substitute, melted

1 teaspoon sea salt

1 tablespoon granulated sugar

To make the crème, combine the banana, brown sugar, soy creamer, and vegan butter substitute in a food processor or blender and process until completely smooth. Pour into a saucepan and cook on medium heat, whisking often, until the mixture boils and the sugar is dissolved. Once the mixture reaches 200 degrees F or begins to boil vigorously, cook without stirring for 8 minutes. Pour into a bowl and cool, stirring occasionally.

Process the tofu in a blender or food processor until smooth and fluffy, about 2 minutes. Stir into the cooled mixture and refrigerate for 4 to 12 hours.

To make the pecans, preheat the oven to 325 degrees F. Place the pecans and vegan butter substitute in a bowl and stir until the pecans are evenly coated. Arrange the pecans on a baking sheet and sprinkle with ½ teaspoon of the salt. Bake for about 15 minutes, or until lightly browned. Sprinkle with the remaining ½ teaspoon of salt and all of the sugar. Cool completely. (The pecans may be roasted up to 2 days in advance, cooled, and stored in an airtight container at room temperature.)

Note: Although the caramel crème topping must be prepared several hours in advance and the assembled cake needs to be refrigerated for an hour or two before serving, this recipe is worth the extra effort. You can make the cake with all of the toppings listed below, or you can use any of the frostings in the book to create your own favorite combinations.

BANANA CAKE

2 ¼ cups all-purpose flour

2 teaspoons baking powder

¾ teaspoon ground cinnamon (optional)

½ teaspoon baking soda

1 cup mashed ripe bananas (about 2 bananas)

½ cup vegan butter substitute, at room temperature

1 ½ cups granulated sugar

1 cup soymilk

2 teaspoons white vinegar

1 teaspoon vanilla extract

FILLING

¼ cup raw cashews

¾ cup silken tofu, well drained

½ cup powdered sugar

1 teaspoon cornstarch

1 teaspoon vanilla extract

1 teaspoon lemon juice

LIME-RUM SPRITZ

2 tablespoons lime juice

2 tablespoons rum

FROSTING

1 recipe Chocolate Frosting (page 23)

GARNISH

2 bananas, sliced

Ground walnuts (optional)

Sliced fresh fruit or berries (optional)

To make the cake, preheat the oven to 350 degrees F and oil and flour two 8-inch round cake pans. Combine the flour, baking powder, optional cinnamon, and baking soda in a bowl. Combine the bananas and vegan butter substitute in a separate large bowl and beat with an electric mixer until creamy. Add the sugar and beat until fluffy. Beat in the soymilk, vinegar, and vanilla extract. Add the flour mixture and stir until just combined. Pour evenly into the prepared pans. Bake for about 30 minutes, or until the top is golden brown, the center bounces back when lightly pressed with a finger, and a toothpick inserted into the center comes out clean. Cool on racks.

To make the filling, while the cake is baking, finely grind the cashews in a food processor. Add the tofu, sugar, cornstarch, vanilla extract, and lemon juice and process until creamy. Chill in the refrigerator until the cakes are cool.

To make the spritz, combine the lime juice and rum in a bowl.

To assemble, remove the cooled cakes from the pans and slice each one in half horizontally with a long knife to make 4 layers in all. Drizzle an equal amount of the Lime-Rum Spritz over each layer. Stir the chilled filling and spread it over 2 of the layers. Spread the Banana Caramel Crème over the remaining 2 layers and evenly arrange the banana slices on top.

Alternate the layers, placing one on top of the other, to create a 4-layer cake. Spread the frosting over the top and sides of the cake. Sprinkle with ground walnuts, if desired, and the pecans. Decorate with fresh fruit, if desired. Refrigerate the assembled cake, uncovered, for 1 to 2 hours before serving. Leftovers should be covered and stored in the refrigerator.

Banana Cupcakes: Oil and flour 15 standard muffin cups or use paper liners. Pour the cake batter evenly into the prepared cups and bake for 25 minutes, or until a toothpick inserted into the center comes out clean. Cool and frost. Makes 15 cupcakes.

How to Make Additional Cake Layers: It's easy to make additional layers with any two-layer cake recipe. Simply slice each cake in half horizontally using a long knife. Double the frosting recipe to be sure you will have enough for all of the additional layers.

Everyone needs a delicious, basic cake. This one can be dressed up any which way you like, or you can turn it into cupcakes.

delicious vanilla cake

*NUT FREE

YIELD: 12 SERVINGS

2 ½ cups all-purpose flour

2 teaspoons baking powder

½ teaspoon baking soda

2 cups powdered sugar

½ cup vegan butter substitute, at room temperature

1 ¾ cups soymilk

2 tablespoons lemon juice

2 teaspoons grated lemon peel

1 tablespoon vanilla extract

1 teaspoon white vinegar

Preheat the oven to 350 degrees F and oil and flour two 8-inch round cake pans. Combine the flour, baking powder, and baking soda in a bowl. In a separate large bowl, combine the sugar and vegan butter substitute and beat with a wooden spoon until smooth. Beat in the soymilk, lemon juice, lemon peel, vanilla extract, and vinegar. Stir in the flour mixture and mix until just combined, making sure there are no lumps.

Pour evenly into the prepared pans. Bake for about 25 minutes, or until lightly browned and a toothpick inserted into the center comes out clean. Cool on racks.

Black and White Cupcakes:
Oil and flour 18 standard muffin cups or use paper liners. Pour the cake batter evenly into the prepared cups and bake for 23 minutes, or until a toothpick inserted into the center comes out clean. Cool and frost with Chocolate Frosting (page 23). Makes 18 cupcakes.

I have a love affair with coconut. On our trips to Jamaica, my husband and I would park ourselves at the tiki bar each afternoon, and our Jamaican friend would climb up a one-hundred-foot-high palm tree to get fresh coconuts for us. He used an ax to open them up just enough to insert a straw, and we would savor the electrolyte-laden juice, which is rumored to have special potency powers.

coconut heaven cake with coconut buttercream frosting

*NUT FREE

YIELD: 12 SERVINGS

COCONUT CAKE

2 ½ cups all-purpose flour

2 teaspoons baking powder

½ teaspoon baking soda

2 cups powdered sugar

½ cup vegan butter substitute, at room temperature

1 ¾ cups soymilk

2 tablespoons lemon juice

2 tablespoons coconut extract

1 teaspoon vanilla extract

1 teaspoon white vinegar

½ cup shredded dried coconut
(unsweetened or sweetened;
if using unsweetened, add
2 tablespoons powdered sugar)

COCONUT BUTTERCREAM FROSTING

4 cups powdered sugar

1 ⅓ cups vegan butter substitute, slightly softened but not at room temperature

2 ½ teaspoons coconut extract

GARNISH

½ cup shredded dried coconut
(sweetened or unsweetened)

To make the cake, preheat the oven to 350 degrees F and oil and flour two 8-inch round cake pans. Combine the flour, baking powder, and baking soda in a bowl. In a separate large bowl, combine the sugar and vegan butter substitute and beat with an electric mixer until smooth. Stir in the soymilk, lemon juice, extracts, and vinegar with a wooden spoon. Add the flour mixture and stir until just combined. Fold in the coconut. Pour evenly into the prepared pans and bake for about 30 minutes, or until a toothpick inserted into the center comes out clean. Cool on racks.

To make the frosting, combine the sugar, vegan butter substitute, and coconut extract in a food processor and process until fluffy. Alternatively, beat with an electric mixer until fluffy. Refrigerate until ready to use.

To assemble, remove the cooled cakes from the pans and spread about one-third of the frosting over 1 of the cakes. Place the other cake on top and frost the top and sides with the remaining frosting. Garnish with the coconut. Store the assembled cake uncovered in the refrigerator and bring to room temperature before serving. Leftovers should be covered and stored in the refrigerator.

This is a lemon lover's must-eat treat! This loaf cake is rich, moist, and refreshing and will surprise you with its tanginess.

lemon-poppy zing cake

LEMON-POPPY ZING CAKE

1½ cups all-purpose flour

3 tablespoons poppy seeds

1 teaspoon baking powder

½ teaspoon baking soda

¼ teaspoon salt

1 cup granulated sugar

⅓ cup vegan butter substitute, at room temperature

1 cup soymilk

2 tablespoons candied lemon peel (optional)

1½ to 2 tablespoons finely grated lemon peel

1 tablespoon lemon juice

1 teaspoon white vinegar

1 teaspoon lemon extract

LEMON GLAZE

2 tablespoons granulated sugar

2 tablespoons lemon juice

1 teaspoon finely grated lemon peel

To make the cake, preheat the oven to 350 degrees F and oil a 9-inch loaf pan. Combine the flour, poppy seeds, baking powder, baking soda, and salt in a bowl. In a separate large bowl, combine the sugar and vegan butter substitute and beat with an electric mixer until smooth. Stir in the soymilk, optional candied lemon peel, grated lemon peel, lemon juice, vinegar, and lemon extract with a wooden spoon. Add the flour mixture and stir until just combined. Pour into the prepared loaf pan and bake for about 45 minutes, or until the center bounces back when lightly pressed with a finger and a toothpick inserted into the center comes out clean. Cool on a rack.

    To make the glaze, combine the sugar and lemon juice in a microwave-safe bowl and microwave at medium power for 45 seconds. Alternatively, heat the sugar and lemon juice in a small saucepan on low heat and stir until the sugar is dissolved. Stir in the lemon peel. Remove the cooled cake from the pan and drizzle the glaze over it. Store covered at room temperature or in the refrigerator (for longer storage).

Lemon-Poppy Zing Muffins: Oil and flour 12 standard muffin cups or use paper liners. Pour the cake batter evenly into the prepared cups and bake for 20 to 22 minutes, or until a toothpick inserted into the center comes out clean. Cool and glaze.

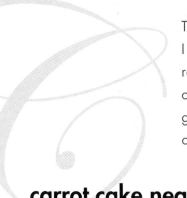

This exotic carrot cake is super moist and full of the delicious surprises I enjoy when visiting Jamaica. *Shumi*, the name of the frosting in this recipe, is a Czech word for the sound the ocean spray makes as waves cascade over land. The frosting is very rich and creamy; no one would guess that it doesn't contain dairy cream cheese. Another welcome aspect of this cake is that you can mix all the ingredients in one bowl.

carrot cake negril

*CAN BE NUT FREE

YIELD: 18 SERVINGS

CARROT CAKE

2 ¼ cups all-purpose flour

1 tablespoon baking powder

1 teaspoon baking soda

½ teaspoon salt

1 cup granulated sugar

1 cup canola oil

¾ cup maple syrup

⅓ cup soymilk

2 tablespoons applesauce

2 teaspoons ground cinnamon

1 teaspoon ground nutmeg

1 teaspoon vanilla extract

2 cups finely grated carrots

1 can (20 ounces) **crushed pineapple, well drained**

¾ cup shredded dried coconut (sweetened or unsweetened)

½ cup chopped walnuts (optional)

⅓ cup raisins

2 tablespoons chopped candied ginger (optional)

2 tablespoons chopped dried orange peel (optional)

WHITE SHUMI FROSTING

1 ⅓ cups powdered sugar

1 cup soy cream cheese

⅓ cup vegan butter substitute, at room temperature

1 teaspoon vanilla extract

To make the cake, preheat the oven to 350 degrees F and oil a 9 x 13-inch baking pan. Combine the flour, baking powder, baking soda, and salt in a large bowl. Add the sugar, oil, maple syrup, soymilk, applesauce, cinnamon, nutmeg, and vanilla extract and stir until combined. Add the carrots, pineapple, coconut, optional walnuts, raisins, and optional candied ginger and orange peel and mix until evenly distributed. Pour into the prepared pan and bake for 45 minutes, or until a toothpick inserted into the center comes out clean. Cool in the baking pan.

To make the frosting, combine all the ingredients in a food processor or blender and process until smooth. Chill before using.

To assemble, spread the chilled frosting over the cooled cake. Cover and store the frosted cake in the refrigerator.

Zucchini have a sense of humor. After a big rain, a foot-long one will pop out of the garden overnight. Of course, I had to create a recipe to help me use up this prolific vegetable. This isn't your typical zucchini bread— it's moist and has an exciting citrus twist. For children who won't eat anything green, it's a great way to get them to love their veggies.

zucchini loaf cake with a tangerine twist

*CAN BE NUT FREE   YIELD: 10 SERVINGS

ZUCCHINI LOAF CAKE

1⅔ cups all-purpose flour

1 teaspoon baking powder

½ teaspoon baking soda

¼ teaspoon salt

1¼ cups granulated sugar

½ cup soymilk

¼ cup canola oil

2 tablespoons tangerine
or orange juice, strained

1 teaspoon white vinegar

1 teaspoon vanilla extract

1 teaspoon ground cinnamon

¼ teaspoon ground cloves

¼ teaspoon ground nutmeg

⅔ cup grated zucchini, packed
(about 1 small)

½ cup chopped walnuts
(optional)

TANGERINE GLAZE

¼ cup granulated sugar

¼ cup tangerine or orange
juice, strained

1 tablespoon finely grated
tangerine or orange peel

1 teaspoon rum or orange
liqueur (optional)

To make the cake, preheat the oven to 350 degrees F and oil and flour a 9-inch loaf pan. Combine the flour, baking powder, baking soda, and salt in a bowl. In a separate large bowl, combine the sugar, soymilk, oil, juice, vinegar, vanilla extract, cinnamon, cloves, and nutmeg and whisk until fluffy. Stir in the flour mixture until just combined. Fold in the zucchini and optional walnuts. Pour into the prepared loaf pan and bake for 50 minutes, or until a toothpick inserted into the center comes out clean. Cool on a rack.

To make the glaze, combine all the ingredients in a microwave-safe bowl and microwave at medium power for about 30 seconds. Alternatively, warm the ingredients in a small saucepan on low heat. Stir until the sugar dissolves. Remove the cooled cake from the pan and spread the glaze on top.

Note: Cover and store the glazed cake in the refrigerator. For longer storage, wrap the unglazed cake tightly in plastic wrap and freeze it for up to two weeks. Thaw at room temperature; glaze it after it has fully thawed.

I'm crazy for homemade candied orange peel, a confection that my mother perfected decades ago. If you also love the tartness of orange combined with chocolate, this is the decadent dessert for you. Choose either frosting, or use both for a multitiered orange sensation!

zesty orange layer cake
with orange buttercream or chocolate-orange frosting

YIELD: 12 SERVINGS

ORANGE CAKE

2 cups all-purpose flour

2 tablespoons finely chopped candied orange peel

1 tablespoon finely grated orange peel

2 teaspoons baking powder

½ teaspoon baking soda

1¼ cups powdered sugar

½ cup vegan butter substitute, at room temperature

⅔ cup soymilk

⅓ cup orange juice

2 teaspoons white vinegar

1 teaspoon orange extract

1 teaspoon vanilla extract

To make the cake, preheat the oven to 350 degrees F and oil two 8-inch round cake pans. Combine the flour, candied orange peel, grated orange peel, baking powder, and baking soda in a bowl. In a separate large bowl, combine the sugar and vegan butter substitute and beat with a wooden spoon until smooth. Beat in the soymilk, orange juice, vinegar, and extracts. Add the flour mixture and stir until just combined. Pour the batter evenly into the prepared pans. Bake for 30 to 35 minutes, or until a toothpick inserted into the center comes out clean. Cool on racks.

ORANGE BUTTERCREAM FROSTING

1 cup powdered sugar

½ cup vegan butter substitute, at room temperature

½ cup soy cream cheese

1 tablespoon finely grated orange peel

1 teaspoon vanilla extract

1 teaspoon orange extract

CHOCOLATE-ORANGE FROSTING

1 cup nondairy chocolate chips

3 tablespoons vegan butter substitute

2 teaspoons orange extract

GARNISH

Orange wedges or candied orange peel

To make the Orange Buttercream Frosting, combine all the ingredients in a bowl and beat with an electric mixer until smooth. Alternatively, combine all the ingredients in a food processor and process until fluffy. Refrigerate until ready to use.

To make the Chocolate-Orange Frosting, melt the chocolate chips and vegan butter substitute in a double boiler over gently simmering water. Alternatively, place them in a microwave-safe bowl and microwave at medium power for 1 minute. Stir. Microwave for 25 seconds longer and stir until smooth. If necessary, microwave for an additional 25 seconds. Stir in the orange extract and keep stirring until the mixture is smooth.

To assemble, remove the cooled cakes from the pans. If you want additional layers, slice each cake in half horizontally with a long knife to make 4 layers. Spread the frosting of your choice over the top of each layer. Arrange the layers on top of each other and frost the sides of the cake with the frosting of your choice. Garnish with orange slices and/or candied orange peel. Cover loosely and store in the refrigerator.

Note: Each frosting recipe makes enough to frost the sides of the cake or the tops of two layers. Double the recipe if you are using four layers, or make both frostings and use one between the layers and the other to frost the sides of the cake.

strawberry fields cake with unbeetable buttercream frosting, page 37

My vegan take on strawberry shortcake is a really simple way to dress up Delicious Vanilla Cake to impress your guests. Try it when extra-sweet strawberries are in season. I invented the colorful frosting out of necessity. I had to make Valentine's Day cupcakes for my son's school and I didn't want to use food coloring, so I relied on the power of beets for a brilliant effect.

strawberry fields cake with unbeetable buttercream frosting

*NUT FREE

YIELD: 12 SERVINGS

UNBEETABLE BUTTERCREAM FROSTING

4 cups powdered sugar

1⅓ cups vegan butter substitute, slightly softened but not at room temperature

2 tablespoons plus 2 teaspoons beet juice (use canned or fresh juice)

1¼ teaspoons vanilla extract

STRAWBERRY FIELDS CAKE

1 recipe Delicious Vanilla Cake (page 28), prepared in two 8-inch round cake pans

2 pounds fresh strawberries, hulled and sliced

To make the frosting, combine all the ingredients in a food processor or blender and process until creamy. Refrigerate until ready to use.

To assemble, remove the cooled cakes from the pans. Spread about one-third of the frosting over 1 of the cakes and arrange half of the strawberries over it. Place the second layer on top of the strawberries and spread the remaining frosting over the top and sides of the cake. Decorate the top and sides of the cake with the remaining strawberries. Cover and store in the refrigerator. Serve as soon as possible.

Note: You can prepare the frosting up to a day in advance. Spoon it into a large zipper-lock plastic bag and store it in the refrigerator. When you are ready to frost the cake, cut a small slit in a corner of the bag and squeeze the frosting onto the cake.

Peaches have a distinctive flavor that blends sweetness and tanginess, adding a bit of surprise to this coffee cake. My family—kids and all—are wild for it, as is every coffee-cake enthusiast who has tasted it. It is great for breakfast as well as dessert. Serve it plain or with Lemon Crème (page 133) on the side.

peach crumb cake

*NUT FREE   YIELD: 12 SERVINGS

PEACH CAKE

2 ¼ cups all-purpose flour

2 teaspoons baking powder

½ teaspoon baking soda

¼ teaspoon salt

1 ⅓ cups granulated sugar

½ cup vegan butter substitute, at room temperature

1 ⅓ cups soymilk

2 teaspoons white vinegar

2 teaspoons finely grated orange peel

2 teaspoons lemon juice

1 teaspoon vanilla extract

½ teaspoon ground cinnamon

2 ½ cups sliced fresh peaches, or 2 cups canned peaches

CRUMB TOPPING

⅓ cup granulated sugar

¼ cup all-purpose flour

1 teaspoon ground cinnamon

2 tablespoons vegan butter substitute, cold

To make the cake, preheat the oven to 350 degrees F and oil and flour a 13 x 9-inch baking pan. Drain the liquid from the peaches in a colander for 30 minutes. Then gently pat the peaches dry with a paper towel. Cut the peaches into ½-inch cubes.

Combine the flour, baking powder, baking soda, and salt in a bowl. In a separate large bowl, combine the sugar and vegan butter substitute and beat with a wooden spoon until smooth. Beat in the soymilk, vinegar, orange peel, lemon juice, vanilla extract, and cinnamon. Stir in the flour mixture until evenly combined. Gently fold in the peaches. Pour the batter into the prepared pan.

To make the topping, combine the sugar, flour, and cinnamon in a bowl. Cut in the vegan butter substitute with a knife, pastry blender, or electric mixer (the mixture will be chunky). Sprinkle over the batter. Bake for about 45 minutes, or until a toothpick inserted into the center comes out clean. Cool on a rack. Store leftover cake tightly covered in the refrigerator.

This wonderfully moist cake is an adaptation of the traditional Israeli New Year cake, which skillfully showcases the apple. The level of tanginess depends on which apples you select. Granny Smith apples make for the strongest flavor, and the contrast between the tart apples and sweet cake is scrumptious. Try serving it with vanilla soy ice cream.

festive apple cake

*CAN BE MADE NUT FREE

YIELD: 12 SERVINGS

1½ cups all-purpose flour

2 teaspoons baking powder

½ teaspoon baking soda

1 cup granulated sugar

½ cup vegan butter substitute, at room temperature

½ cup soymilk

2 tablespoons maple syrup

2 teaspoons white or cider vinegar

1 teaspoon ground cinnamon

1 teaspoon finely grated orange peel

5 cups peeled and sliced apples (about 5 medium apples)

⅓ cup chopped walnuts (optional)

⅓ cup raisins (optional)

½ teaspoon ground nutmeg (optional)

Preheat the oven to 350 degrees F and oil a 9-inch springform pan. Combine the flour, baking powder, and baking soda in a bowl. In a separate large bowl, combine the sugar and vegan butter substitute and beat with a wooden spoon until smooth. Beat in the soymilk, maple syrup, vinegar, cinnamon, and orange peel. Add the flour mixture and stir until just combined. Gently fold in the apples and the optional walnuts, raisins, and nutmeg. Pour into the prepared pan and bake for 1 hour and 5 minutes, or until the top is golden brown and a toothpick inserted into the center comes out clean. Cool on a rack. Store leftover cake tightly covered in the refrigerator.

Pear Cake: Replace the apples with 5 cups peeled and sliced pears (about 6 medium pears). If the pears are very juicy, blot them with paper towels before folding them into the batter.

Note: You can use a single kind or a combination of apples. If using Granny Smith apples or other apples that are extra tart, add an extra tablespoon of maple syrup. Any apples except Red Delicious will work in this recipe.

This cake contains all the fabulous flavors of the candy we love. It's absolute heaven.

ultimate peanut butter cup cake

YIELD: 12 SERVINGS

PEANUT BUTTER CUP CAKE

2 ⅓ cups all-purpose flour

2 teaspoons baking powder

½ teaspoon baking soda

¼ teaspoon salt

1½ cups granulated sugar

½ cup unsalted creamy peanut butter

⅓ cup vegan butter substitute, at room temperature

1 cup soymilk

¼ cup applesauce

2 teaspoons white vinegar

1 teaspoon vanilla extract

CHOCOLATE–PEANUT BUTTER FROSTING

1 cup nondairy chocolate chips

1 cup unsalted creamy peanut butter

½ cup powdered sugar, sifted

⅓ cup vegan butter substitute, at room temperature

To make the cake, preheat the oven to 350 degrees F and oil and flour two 8-inch round cake pans. Combine the flour, baking powder, baking soda, and salt in a bowl. In a separate large bowl, combine the sugar, peanut butter, and vegan butter substitute and beat with an electric mixer until fluffy. Beat in the soymilk, applesauce, vinegar, and vanilla extract. Add the flour mixture and stir until just combined. Bake for 25 to 28 minutes, or until a toothpick inserted into the center comes out clean. Cool on racks.

To make the frosting, melt the chocolate chips in a double boiler over gently simmering water. Alternatively, place them in a microwave-safe bowl and microwave at medium power for 1 minute. Stir. Microwave for 25 seconds longer and stir until smooth. If necessary, microwave for an additional 25 seconds. Combine the melted chocolate with the peanut butter, powdered sugar, and vegan butter substitute in a food processor or blender and process until smooth and fluffy. Alternatively, beat with an electric mixer.

To assemble, remove the cooled cakes from the pans and spread about one-third of the frosting over 1 of the cakes. Place the other cake over it and frost the top and sides. Cover and store in the refrigerator until serving time.

This is a tender, tasty cake that you can dress up beautifully. Use the tastiest organic raspberry preserves you can find, as its flavor will be a perfect contrast to the cake and the other toppings.

almond-raspberry cake
with ganache and almond buttercream frosting

YIELD: 12 SERVINGS

ALMOND-RASPBERRY CAKE

2 ⅓ cups all-purpose flour

2 teaspoons baking powder

½ teaspoon baking soda

2 cups powdered sugar

½ cup vegan butter substitute, at room temperature

1¾ cups soymilk or almond milk

2 tablespoons lemon juice

2 tablespoons unsalted creamy almond butter

2 tablespoons almond extract

1 teaspoon white vinegar

1 teaspoon vanilla extract

RASPBERRY SAUCE

½ cup raspberry preserves

1 tablespoon granulated sugar

1 tablespoon water

To make the cake, preheat the oven to 350 degrees F and oil and flour two 8-inch round cake pans. Combine the flour, baking powder, and baking soda in a bowl. In a separate large bowl, combine the sugar and vegan butter substitute and beat with an electric mixer until fluffy. Beat in the soymilk, lemon juice, almond butter, almond extract, vinegar, and vanilla extract. Add the flour mixture and stir with a wooden spoon until just combined. Pour evenly into the prepared pans. Bake for about 30 minutes, or until a toothpick inserted into the center comes out clean. Cool on racks.

To make the sauce, combine the raspberry preserves, sugar, and water in a small saucepan. Bring to a boil, stirring constantly, and simmer for 3 minutes. Alternatively, place the ingredients in a microwave-safe bowl and microwave at medium power for 30 seconds. Strain the mixture through a fine-mesh strainer.

GANACHE

½ cup nondairy chocolate chips

¼ cup soy creamer or soymilk

½ teaspoon instant coffee granules

ALMOND BUTTERCREAM FROSTING

1¾ cups powdered sugar

½ cup vegan butter substitute, slightly softened but not at room temperature

¾ teaspoon almond extract

GARNISH

Slivered or sliced almonds

Fresh raspberries

To make the ganache, combine the chocolate chips, soy creamer, and instant coffee granules in a double boiler over gently simmering water until melted. Alternatively, place the ingredients in a microwave-safe bowl and microwave at medium power for 1 minute. Stir. Microwave for 25 seconds longer and stir until smooth. If necessary, microwave for an additional 25 seconds.

To make the frosting, combine all the ingredients in a blender or food processor and process until creamy. Refrigerate before using, if time permits.

To assemble, remove the cooled cakes from the pans and spread about one-third of the frosting over 1 of the cakes. Carefully spread all of the sauce on top of the frosting. Let stand until the sauce has firmed up slightly, up to 1 hour. Place the other cake over it and spread the ganache on top. Frost the sides with the remaining frosting. If there is any frosting left over, pipe designs on top of the cake. Garnish with almonds and raspberries. Store in the refrigerator.

Note: If you make the ganache in advance, you might need to reheat it so it will be spreadable.

A decadent, super-sweet, traditional English treat, this isn't like an American pudding. It's a moist date cake with a rich toffee sauce that you serve warm over it. For an extra-special treat, top it with vanilla soy ice cream or any crème of your choice.

sticky toffee pudding

DATE MIXTURE

2 cups chopped dates

2 cups water

CAKE

3 cups all-purpose flour

1 teaspoon baking powder

½ teaspoon baking soda

½ teaspoon salt

2 cups powdered sugar

½ cup vegan butter substitute, at room temperature

¼ cup soymilk

1 teaspoon white vinegar

STICKY SAUCE

2½ cups brown sugar

1 cup vegan butter substitute

1 cup vanilla soy creamer, or 1 cup plain soy creamer plus ½ teaspoon vanilla extract

To make the Date Mixture, combine the dates and water in a small saucepan and simmer until the dates soften, about 5 minutes. Set aside to cool; do not drain. When cool, process in a blender or food processor until smooth.

To make the cake, preheat the oven to 350 degrees F and oil and flour a 9 x 13-inch baking pan. Combine the flour, baking powder, baking soda, and salt in a bowl. In a separate large bowl, combine the sugar and vegan butter substitute and beat with a wooden spoon until fluffy. Beat in the soymilk and vinegar. Stir in the flour mixture and Date Mixture and mix until smooth. Pour the batter into the prepared pan. Bake for about 35 minutes, or until the cake is light brown and a toothpick inserted into the center comes out clean.

To make the sauce, combine the sugar, vegan butter substitute, and half of the soy creamer in a medium saucepan and mix well. Bring to a boil, stirring often with a wooden spoon. Remove from the heat and let cool slightly. Whisk in the remaining soy creamer. If you are using plain creamer, stir in the vanilla extract.

To serve, poke many holes in the top of the cake using a fork and pour half of the sauce over the top, allowing it to soak into the cake. Cut the cake into 3-inch squares. Keep the remaining sauce hot and spoon it over the warm cake. Store leftover sauce and cake tightly covered in the refrigerator.

Note: You can prepare the Sticky Sauce a day in advance; just mix it well prior to serving as it may separate. You can also make the cake a day in advance. Before serving, warm it for 5 to 10 minutes in a preheated oven at 350 degrees F. For fewer servings, you can easily cut the recipe in half and use a 9-inch square baking pan. The baking time will remain the same.

As a child, I incessantly perused old cookbooks for fun. Uniquely beautiful roll cakes particularly intrigued me. If you have ever tasted cashew butter or cashew-macadamia butter, you know how sumptuous it is. The complementary flavors of coconut and lemon are paired in this incredibly rich, creamy, and moist roll cake.

cashew-coconut-lemon roll cake

YIELD: 16 SERVINGS

CASHEW-COCONUT-LEMON CAKE

2 cups all-purpose flour

2 teaspoons baking powder

½ teaspoon baking soda

½ teaspoon salt

1 cup granulated sugar

½ cup unsalted creamy cashew or cashew-macadamia butter

1¼ cups soymilk

2 tablespoons canola oil

1 teaspoon cider vinegar

1 tablespoon lemon juice

1 teaspoon vanilla extract

1 teaspoon lemon extract

½ teaspoon coconut extract

½ cup shredded dried coconut (sweetened or unsweetened)

To make the cake, preheat the oven to 350 degrees F and line an 18 x 13 x 1-inch jelly roll pan with parchment paper. Spray the parchment paper with canola oil spray.

Combine the flour, baking powder, baking soda, and salt in a bowl. In a separate large bowl, combine the sugar and cashew butter and beat with a wooden spoon until smooth. Beat in the soymilk, oil, vinegar, lemon juice, and extracts. Add the flour mixture and coconut and stir until just combined. Pour evenly into the prepared pan. Bake for about 18 minutes, or until the cake puffs up and turns a very light golden brown and a toothpick inserted into the center comes out clean. Cool on a rack for 10 minutes.

CASHEW FILLING

1 ½ cups firm silken tofu, well drained

1 cup shredded dried coconut (sweetened or unsweetened)

½ cup unsalted creamy cashew or cashew-macadamia butter

½ cup powdered sugar

½ cup maple syrup

½ cup soy cream cheese

1 tablespoon lemon juice

1 tablespoon cornstarch

2 ½ teaspoons finely grated lemon peel

1 teaspoon lemon extract

½ teaspoon coconut extract

GARNISHES (optional)

Unsweetened cocoa powder

½ cup shredded dried coconut (sweetened or unsweetened)

To make the filling, combine all the ingredients in a food processor and process until creamy and smooth. Refrigerate the filling while the cake is baking.

To assemble, carefully remove the cake from the pan. Cut off all the edges. Spread the top with a ¼-inch layer of the filling. Sprinkle the filling with cocoa powder, if desired, and roll up the cake very carefully. Cover the cake with part or all of the remaining filling and garnish with the coconut, if desired. Alternatively, pipe designs with any remaining frosting using a pastry bag. Store uncovered in the refrigerator until serving time. Store leftovers covered in the refrigerator.

Note: If you want to use the filling for the top and sides of the cake, prepare an additional half of the recipe. If you want a chocolate top, use Chocolate Frosting (page 23) instead of the Cashew Filling.

This hearty carrot cake is spicy and has a smooth texture; it's more cakey and less chunky than Carrot Cake Negril (page 31). My husband is nuts for it and even packs some to take on business trips. Cut it into squares and take some to go.

carrot spice cake

*CAN BE NUT FREE   YIELD: 12 SERVINGS

1⅓ cups all-purpose flour

1 teaspoon baking powder

½ teaspoon baking soda

½ teaspoon salt

1 cup granulated sugar

½ cup vegan butter substitute, at room temperature

⅓ cup soymilk

¼ cup applesauce

2 teaspoons ground cinnamon

1 teaspoon vanilla extract

½ teaspoon ground nutmeg

1 cup finely grated carrots

1 cup chopped walnuts (optional)

Powdered sugar or White Shumi Frosting (page 31; optional)

Preheat the oven to 350 degrees F and oil a 9-inch square baking pan. Combine the flour, baking powder, baking soda, and salt in a bowl. In a separate large bowl, combine the sugar and vegan butter substitute and beat with a wooden spoon until smooth. Beat in the soymilk, applesauce, cinnamon, vanilla extract, and nutmeg. Stir in the flour mixture until just combined. Fold in the carrots and optional walnuts. Pour into the prepared pan and bake for 50 minutes, or until a toothpick inserted in the center comes out clean. Cool on a rack.

If desired, dust with powdered sugar or use a pastry bag to pipe designs using White Shumi Frosting.

Note: For an even finer texture, grate or finely chop the carrots in a food processor. Watch closely so they are not puréed.

Don't make these if you don't mean business. I'm a testament to the power of these muffins. I left a dozen at my husband's doorstep soon after we started dating and look what happened! They worked well for me, and they might serve you well too. Amorous outcomes aside, you are certain to have fun eating these moist little cakes that mix up in one bowl.

pumpkin–chocolate chip muffins

*CAN BE NUT FREE

YIELD: 12 MUFFINS

1 cup all-purpose flour

1 teaspoon baking powder

1 teaspoon ground cinnamon

½ teaspoon baking soda

1 can (16 ounces) pumpkin

1 cup granulated sugar

½ cup canola oil

⅓ cup soymilk

¾ cup nondairy chocolate chips

½ cup chopped walnuts (optional)

Preheat the oven to 350 degrees F and oil a standard 12-cup muffin pan or line it with paper liners. Combine the flour, baking powder, cinnamon, and baking soda in a large bowl. Add the pumpkin, sugar, oil, and soymilk and stir until just combined. Gently stir in the chocolate chips and optional walnuts. Spoon evenly into the prepared muffin cups. Bake for 25 minutes, or until a toothpick inserted into the center of a muffin comes out clean.

very berry corn muffins, page 51

pumpkin—chocolate chip muffins, page 49

Since I tasted the packaged variety as a kid, I've always loved corn muffins. It was imperative for me to create a fluffy, tasty muffin that didn't have the grease of the typical store-bought corn muffins. For an extra treat, I spread these with coconut oil. Sunday mornings just aren't complete in my house without a batch of these quick-and-easy muffins with a berry twist. Who needs pancakes?

very berry corn muffins

YIELD: 12 MUFFINS

1¼ cup all-purpose flour

¾ cup yellow cornmeal

⅓ cup granulated sugar

2 teaspoons baking powder

½ teaspoons baking soda

¼ teaspoon salt

1 cup soymilk

⅓ cup canola oil

1 tablespoon grated orange peel (or peel from 1 orange)

¾ to 1 cup fresh, frozen, or dried mixed berries or blueberries

Preheat the oven to 400 degrees and oil a standard 12-cup muffin pan or line it with paper liners. Combine the flour, cornmeal, sugar, baking powder, baking soda, and salt in a large bowl. Add the soymilk, canola oil, and orange peel and stir to combine. Fold in the berries. Spoon the batter evenly into the prepared muffin cups.

Bake for 18 to 20 minutes, or until the tops are lightly browned and a toothpick inserted in the center of a muffin comes out clean. Cool on racks. Store in a sealed container at room temperature.

Scrumptious COOKIES

Cookies were challenging for me when I started baking vegan treats. But once I got the hang of the basic steps and found the right ingredients to use, I quickly learned that making great vegan cookies really is a piece of cake!

This chapter lays it all out for you. The following tips provide the information you need to succeed at creating the best vegan cookies to suit the tastes of your friends and family. From the basic chocolate chip cookie to the more complex flavors of a sandwich cookie, I'm sure you will enjoy this collection. And if you don't tell anyone, no one will guess they are vegan!

sweet utopia tips

THE SECRET TO SUCCESS

Making the best vegan cookies depends predominantly on the vegan butter substitute you use. All of my recipes have been created and tested with Earth Balance, a brand-name buttery-tasting spread that is available in tubs or sticks. Earth Balance has the perfect consistency and taste to replace butter, so I encourage you to use it for the best results with your cookies. Ordinary margarine is not a good choice for vegan cookies, as it will make for a thinner dough, causing the cookies to spread out, flatten, and burn as they bake.

opposite: fudgy chip cookies, page 57

EQUIP YOURSELF

To prevent cookies from burning, use insulated baking sheets. For easier cleanup and also to help prevent burning and sticking, line standard baking sheets with parchment paper. Baking times will vary slightly depending on the type of bakeware you use.

OIL IT

I like to "grease" baking sheets the modern way, using organic vegetable oil spray. Vegetable oil spray makes this task simple and quick, with much less mess than using margarine. I prefer using canola oil spray; look for brands that contain organic canola oil with natural propellants (no chlorofluoro-carbons). If you prefer to use plain canola oil, apply a small amount to a clean cloth or pastry brush and spread a very thin film of it over the baking sheets or pan.

WORKING WITH DOUGH

Chill cookie dough thoroughly, because vegan butter substitute becomes soft quickly. When rolling the dough is required, work quickly. Don't let the dough get too soft or your cookies will spread out too much.

CUT IT OUT

- For cutout cookies, knead the dough into a large ball, wrap it tightly in plastic wrap, and refrigerate it for one to twelve hours; this will make it much easier to work with. If you are making a lot of cookies and the dough starts to get soft again, just put it in the freezer for a little while until it is chilled but not frozen. Let well-chilled dough sit for ten minutes or so at room temperature before using it.

- Flour is your friend when you are rolling cookie dough and cutting out shapes. Use it to dust your work surface and your rolling pin, and flour your hands as necessary as the dough warms and becomes stickier. Dust flour directly on the dough if it becomes sticky.

- When cookie dough for cutout cookies is initially mixed, it should resemble coarse crumbs. Knead the dough briefly to integrate the ingredients better, but be careful not to overknead or the cookies will be tough.

- Place the dough between two sheets of waxed paper and roll it out to one-quarter inch thick.

- For a thinner, crisper cookie, roll the cookie dough out to one-sixth inch thick and bake it for a shorter time.
- There are many places to buy cookie cutters in fun shapes—craft stores, supermarkets, department stores, dollar stores, and many shops that sell cookware and baking supplies.

IS IT DONE YET?

In general, when cookies begin to brown at the edges, they should be taken out of the oven. Some types of cookies are better when they are baked a little longer, until they are golden brown. Others should be baked just until they are set. When in doubt, take them out! It's better to underbake them by a minute than have cookies that are overbaked and rock hard.

FUN BITS

To add crunch or chewiness to cookies, be creative. There's no limit to the types of cookies you can make using various nuts and other additions. If you want to swap raisins for chocolate chips, dried cherries for raisins, or just add dried blueberries, go ahead! Feel free to adjust the amount of additions in a recipe to suit your preference. Your cookies are a reflection of your personality, so if you're nutty, show it!

tahini-coconut-oatmeal cookies, page 60

KEEPING IT FRESH

Cookies are best enjoyed the same day they are baked, especially ones with gooey chocolate chips. Store cookies between sheets of parchment paper in an airtight container to keep them from sticking together. Refrigeration helps cookies stay fresh longer.

Chocolate chip cookies are an all-around comfort food, and they have a sweet spot in the hearts of most adults and kids. Eat them while they're warm and gooey, and try to keep some around for a bit longer, too, if you can!

chocolate chippers

*CAN BE NUT FREE   YIELD: ABOUT 30 COOKIES

2 cups all-purpose flour

½ teaspoon baking soda

¼ teaspoon salt

1 cup vegan butter substitute, slightly softened but not at room temperature

¾ cup brown sugar

⅓ cup granulated sugar

⅓ cup plus 1 tablespoon applesauce

2 tablespoons nondairy milk

1 teaspoon vanilla extract

1 teaspoon almond extract or additional vanilla extract

1 to 1¼ cups nondairy chocolate chips

1 cup chopped nuts of choice (optional)

Preheat the oven to 350 degrees F and oil 3 baking sheets. Combine the flour, baking soda, and salt in a bowl. In a separate large bowl, combine the vegan butter substitute, brown sugar, and granulated sugar and beat with a wooden spoon until fluffy. Beat in the applesauce, nondairy milk, and extracts. Add the flour mixture and stir to combine. Stir in the chocolate chips and optional nuts.

If the dough is very soft, refrigerate it for about 20 minutes. Form the dough into 1½-inch balls and arrange them on the prepared baking sheets about 3 inches apart. Bake for about 16 minutes, or until the cookies just begin to lightly brown. Cool on racks. Store in a sealed container.

These incredibly indulgent, chocolaty cookies are best served warm and chewy, soon after they come out of the oven. Don't let them sit around for long!

fudgy chip cookies

*CAN BE NUT FREE

YIELD: ABOUT 30 COOKIES

2 ¼ cups all-purpose flour

½ cup unsweetened cocoa powder

1 teaspoon baking powder

1½ cups granulated sugar

1 cup vegan butter substitute, slightly softened but not at room temperature

½ cup soymilk

2 teaspoons vanilla extract

1 cup nondairy chocolate chips

⅔ cup chopped nuts of choice (optional)

Preheat the oven to 350 degrees F and oil 3 baking sheets. Sift the flour, cocoa powder, and baking powder into a bowl. In a separate large bowl, combine the sugar and vegan butter substitute and beat with a wooden spoon until creamy. Beat in the soymilk and vanilla extract. Add the flour mixture and stir to combine. Stir in the chocolate chips and optional nuts.

If the dough is very soft, refrigerate it for about 20 minutes. Form the dough into 1½-inch balls using wet hands and arrange them on the prepared baking sheets about 2 inches apart. Press down lightly on each ball so the top is flattened. Bake for 14 to 15 minutes. They will not look as "done" as other cookies, as they will not be firm or dry. Make sure you do not overbake them or they will be hard, not chewy. Cool on racks. Store in a sealed container.

These gooey cookies have a deep coffee aroma and flavor. They are very chewy and soft, especially when just baked.

mocha-almond chippers

2 cups all-purpose flour

¾ teaspoon baking soda

⅛ teaspoon salt

¾ cup vegan butter substitute, slightly softened but not at room temperature

⅔ cup granulated sugar

½ cup brown sugar

⅓ cup soymilk

3 tablespoons instant coffee granules

1 teaspoon vanilla extract

1 teaspoon white vinegar

1 cup nondairy chocolate chips

¾ cup chopped lightly toasted slivered almonds

Preheat the oven to 350 degrees F and oil 3 baking sheets. Combine the flour, baking soda, and salt in a bowl. In a separate large bowl, combine the vegan butter substitute, granulated sugar, and brown sugar and beat with a wooden spoon until smooth. Beat in the soymilk, coffee granules, vanilla extract, and vinegar. Add the flour mixture and stir until combined. Stir in the chocolate chips and almonds.

Form the dough into 1½-inch balls and arrange them on the prepared baking sheets about 3 inches apart. Press down lightly on each ball so the top is flattened. Bake for about 10 minutes, or until the edges begin to lightly brown. Make sure you do not overbake these cookies or they will be hard, not chewy. Let cool on the baking sheets for about 3 minutes before transferring to racks to cool completely. Store in a sealed container.

Chewy and comforting, these oatmeal cookies really satisfy. You get a surprise serving of vegetables in each cookie, though no one (especially kids) will ever suspect it!

green speckled oaties

*NUT FREE

YIELD: ABOUT 30 COOKIES

½ cup soymilk

⅓ cup raisins

⅓ cup fresh spinach or thawed and drained frozen spinach, packed

3 cups rolled oats

2 cups all-purpose flour

1 teaspoon ground cinnamon

¾ teaspoon baking soda

¼ teaspoon salt

⅔ cup vegan butter substitute, slightly softened but not at room temperature

⅔ cup granulated sugar

⅔ cup maple syrup

2 teaspoons vanilla extract

Preheat the oven to 350 degrees F and oil 3 baking sheets. Combine the soymilk and raisins in a small bowl and let soak for 15 to 60 minutes. Transfer the soymilk and raisins to a blender or food processor, add the spinach, and process until just combined. Take care not to purée the mixture; some very small pieces should remain.

Combine the rolled oats, flour, cinnamon, baking soda, and salt in a bowl. In a separate large bowl, combine the vegan butter substitute, sugar, maple syrup, and vanilla extract and beat with a wooden spoon until creamy. Add the spinach mixture and stir until incorporated. Stir in the oat mixture until evenly combined.

Form the dough into 1½ to 2-inch balls and arrange them on the prepared baking sheets about 3 inches apart. Bake for 16 to 18 minutes, or until the edges are golden brown. Cool on racks. Store in a sealed container.

These nourishing balls are not too sweet, and you can easily substitute any other flour you like. Tahini is a very nutritious alternative to butter made from sesame seeds. It is the consistency of peanut butter and is high in protein and beneficial fats.

tahini-coconut-oatmeal cookies

YIELD: ABOUT 24 COOKIES

1 cup all-purpose flour

½ teaspoon baking powder

½ cup tahini

⅓ cup maple syrup or agave syrup

¼ cup granulated sugar

¼ cup soymilk

1 teaspoon vanilla extract

½ teaspoon ground cinnamon

1 cup rolled oats

½ cup chopped walnuts

½ cup shredded dried coconut (sweetened or unsweetened)

⅓ cup powdered sugar (optional)

Preheat the oven to 350 degrees F and oil 3 baking sheets. Combine the flour and baking powder in a bowl. In a separate large bowl, combine the tahini, maple syrup, and granulated sugar and beat with a wooden spoon until creamy. Beat in the soymilk, vanilla extract, and cinnamon. Add the flour mixture and stir until just combined. Mix in the oats, walnuts, and coconut.

Form the dough into 1-inch balls and arrange them on the prepared baking sheets about 2 inches apart. Bake for 13 to 15 minutes, or until the edges are very lightly browned. Cool on racks. Dust the cooled cookies with the powdered sugar, if desired. Store in a sealed container.

Showcased in these cookies is the humble sesame seed. This seed is an excellent source of protein, healthful fat, calcium, and several other nutrients. Sesame's roots run deep: the seed was cultivated in Africa and India as far back as 2250 BC, and it is a staple among many cultures on several continents.

sesame cookies

YIELD: ABOUT 30 COOKIES

⅔ cup raw sesame seeds

2 cups all-purpose flour

¾ teaspoon baking powder

¼ teaspoon salt

⅔ cup granulated sugar

½ cup vegan butter substitute, slightly softened but not at room temperature

¼ cup tahini

⅓ cup plus 1 tablespoon soymilk

1 teaspoon almond extract

1 teaspoon vanilla extract

Preheat the oven to 350 degrees F. Spread the sesame seeds in a thin layer on a dry baking sheet (an insulated baking sheet or a regular baking sheet lined with parchment paper or a silicone pad) and place in the oven for about 5 minutes. Do not let them brown. Immediately transfer the seeds to a bowl.

Oil 3 baking sheets. Combine the flour, baking powder, and salt in a bowl. In a separate large bowl, combine the sugar, vegan butter substitute, and tahini and beat with a wooden spoon until creamy. Beat in the soymilk, extracts, and half of the sesame seeds. Add the flour mixture and stir until combined. Shape the dough into small logs, about 1½ inches long and ¾ inch in diameter. Form the logs into rings, if desired. Roll the logs in the remaining sesame seeds and arrange them on the prepared baking sheets about 2 inches apart. Bake for 16 to 18 minutes, or until the cookies begin to turn light brown. Cool on racks. Store in a sealed container.

If you enjoy a wholesome, cakelike cookie that tastes delicious, you will surely enjoy these. Nutritious nut butter brings out the flavor in these goodies.

banana-cranberry-cashew cookies

YIELD: ABOUT 24 COOKIES

2 cups all-purpose flour

1 teaspoon baking powder

½ teaspoon ground cinnamon

½ teaspoon baking soda

½ teaspoon salt

1 cup mashed ripe banana (about 2 bananas)

¾ cup brown sugar

½ cup vegan butter substitute, slightly softened but not at room temperature

⅓ cup granulated sugar

¼ cup unsalted creamy nut butter (almond, cashew, or macadamia)

1 tablespoon soymilk

1 teaspoon almond extract

¾ cup chopped cashews

⅓ cup dried cranberries

Preheat the oven to 350 degrees F and oil 3 baking sheets. Combine the flour, baking powder, cinnamon, baking soda, and salt in a bowl. In a separate large bowl, combine the banana, brown sugar, vegan butter substitute, granulated sugar, and nut butter and beat with an electric mixer until smooth and fluffy. Beat in the soymilk and almond extract. Add the flour mixture and stir to combine. Stir in the chopped cashews and cranberries.

Drop the dough by 1 tablespoon per cookie onto the prepared baking sheets about 3 inches apart. Bake for 13 to 15 minutes, or until the edges begin to brown. Cool on racks. Store loosely covered in the refrigerator.

Note: Dried cherries make a great substitute for cranberries. You can also use dried blueberries, finely chopped dried apricot pieces, raisins, or other dried or candied fruit. For a spicier cookie, add one-quarter teaspoon ground nutmeg to the flour mixture.

banana-cranberry-cashew cookies, page 62

lemon hearts, page 65

These heart cookies are basic cutouts with a tangy, lemony twist. You can make them thick and soft or thin and crisp to suit your taste. I use fanciful cookie-cutter shapes and a sprinkle of glittery colored sugar to make these a hit with preschoolers.

lemon hearts

*NUT FREE   YIELD: ABOUT 18 COOKIES

LEMON COOKIES

2 cups all-purpose flour

1 teaspoon baking powder

¼ teaspoon salt

1 cup vegan butter substitute, slightly softened but not at room temperature

⅔ cup granulated sugar

3 tablespoons lemon juice

1½ tablespoons grated lemon peel

1 teaspoon lemon extract

1 teaspoon vanilla extract

LEMON GLAZE

2 tablespoons lemon juice

1 tablespoon granulated sugar

GARNISH (optional)

Colored sugar

To make the cookies, combine the flour, baking powder, and salt in a large bowl. In a separate large bowl, combine the vegan butter substitute and sugar and beat with an electric mixer until fluffy. Add the lemon juice, lemon peel, and extracts. Stir in the flour mixture with a wooden spoon until well combined. Gather the dough into a ball, cover with plastic wrap, and refrigerate for 2 to 12 hours.

Preheat the oven to 350 degrees F and oil 3 baking sheets. Roll out the dough on a floured surface to ¼ inch thick. Cut into 3-inch hearts and arrange on the prepared baking sheets 2 inches apart. Bake for 20 minutes, or until the edges start to brown slightly. Check the cookies after 12 minutes to make sure they are baking evenly. If they are not, turn the baking sheets around and continue to bake. Let the cookies cool on the baking sheets for 2 minutes, then transfer to racks to cool completely.

To make the glaze, combine the lemon juice and sugar in a microwave-safe bowl and microwave at medium power for 30 seconds. Stir until the sugar is dissolved. Alternatively, warm the lemon juice and sugar in a small saucepan on low heat until the sugar is melted. Brush the glaze over the cooled cookies. Sprinkle with colored sugar, if desired. Store in a sealed container.

Although many people don't believe this, you don't need egg whites to make macaroons! After years of searching for a decent macaroon made without eggs, I created one that is really enjoyable.

almond macaroons

YIELD: ABOUT 30 COOKIES

1 cup all-purpose flour

1 teaspoon baking powder

⅛ teaspoon salt

⅔ cup granulated sugar (increase to 1 cup if using unsweetened coconut)

½ cup plus 1 tablespoon vegan butter substitute, slightly softened but not at room temperature

¼ cup lightly toasted slivered almonds, finely ground in a food processor (do not let them turn into a paste)

1½ tablespoons soy cream cheese

¼ cup soymilk

½ teaspoon almond extract

2¼ cups shredded dried coconut (sweetened or unsweetened), as needed

¼ cup finely chopped lightly toasted slivered almonds

Combine the flour, baking powder, and salt in a bowl. In a separate large bowl, combine the sugar, vegan butter substitute, ground almonds, and soy cream cheese and beat with an electric mixer until blended. Beat in the soymilk and almond extract. Add the flour mixture and mix with a wooden spoon until evenly combined. Stir in the chopped almonds and 2 cups of the coconut. Gather the dough into a ball, cover with plastic wrap, and refrigerate for 2 to 12 hours.

Preheat the oven to 350 degrees F and oil 3 baking sheets. Form the dough into 1-inch balls. Roll the balls in the remaining ¼ cup of coconut, if desired. Place the balls on the prepared baking sheets about 3 inches apart. Bake for 15 minutes, or until the cookies are lightly browned on the bottom and edges. Let cool on the baking sheets for 3 minutes. Transfer to a rack or a flat surface and let cool thoroughly. Store in a sealed container.

Chocolate-Coated Macaroons: Melt ⅓ cup nondairy chocolate chips and 2 teaspoons vegan butter substitute. Mix well. Drizzle in patterns over the cooled cookies.

Not only are these cookies pretty, speckled with poppy seeds and bursts of red cherries and jam, they are super delicious. Feel free to use cranberries or raisins if you can't find dried cherries.

cherry–poppy seed jam prints

*NUT FREE   YIELD: ABOUT 24 COOKIES

2 cups all-purpose flour

2 tablespoons poppy seeds

1 teaspoon baking powder

½ teaspoon baking soda

½ teaspoon salt

1 cup vegan butter substitute, slightly softened but not at room temperature

1 cup powdered sugar

1 tablespoon soymilk

1 teaspoon vanilla extract

1 teaspoon almond extract

½ cup dried cherries, finely chopped

½ cup berry preserves of choice

Combine the flour, poppy seeds, baking powder, baking soda, and salt in a bowl. In a separate large bowl, combine the vegan butter substitute and sugar and beat with an electric mixer until light and fluffy. Beat in the soymilk and extracts. Add the flour mixture and stir to combine. Stir in the dried cherries. Chill the dough for at least 1 hour in the refrigerator so it will be easier to work with.

Preheat the oven to 300 degrees F. Form the dough into 1- to 2-inch balls and arrange them on 3 dry baking sheets about 2 inches apart. With your thumb, make an indentation in the center of each cookie and round off the edges. Using a tiny spoon, fill each indentation with about ½ teaspoon of preserves. Bake for about 10 minutes, or until the edges begin to brown. Transfer immediately to racks and let cool. Store in a sealed container.

These exquisite treats are perfect for those who demand carrot cake. Supplement your party dessert platter with them and spare the mess of a cake.

carrot cake cookies with maple–cream cheese frosting

*CAN BE NUT FREE

YIELD: ABOUT 24 COOKIES

CARROT CAKE COOKIES

1½ cups all-purpose flour

1 teaspoon baking powder

½ teaspoon baking soda

¼ teaspoon salt

½ cup vegan butter substitute, slightly softened but not at room temperature

½ cup brown sugar

½ cup granulated sugar

3 tablespoons soymilk

1 teaspoon vanilla extract

1 teaspoon ground cinnamon

¼ teaspoon ground nutmeg

¼ teaspoon ground ginger

1 cup finely grated carrots (about 2 carrots)

½ cup walnuts, finely chopped (optional)

½ cup raisins, chopped (optional)

MAPLE–CREAM CHEESE FROSTING

½ cup powdered sugar

½ cup soy cream cheese

¼ cup vegan butter substitute, at room temperature

¼ cup maple syrup

1 teaspoon vanilla extract

To make the cookies, preheat the oven to 350 degrees F and oil 3 baking sheets. Combine the flour, baking powder, baking soda, and salt in a bowl. In a separate large bowl, combine the vegan butter substitute, brown sugar, and granulated sugar and beat with a wooden spoon until creamy. Beat in the soymilk, vanilla extract, cinnamon, nutmeg, and ginger. Add the flour mixture and stir until just combined. Stir in the carrots and optional walnuts and raisins.

Drop the dough by 1½ tablespoons per cookie onto the prepared baking sheets about 2 inches apart. Bake for about 18 minutes, until lightly browned and springy to the touch. Cool on the baking sheets for 1 minute, then transfer to racks to cool completely.

To make the frosting, combine all the ingredients in a food processor or blender and process until smooth. Drizzle over the cooled cookies. Store in a sealed container in the refrigerator.

Carrot Cake Sandwich Cookies: Prepare the Maple-Cream Cheese Frosting as directed, increasing the powdered sugar to 1 cup and the soy cream cheese to ¾ cup. Cover and chill in the refrigerator for at least 1 hour. Spread a small amount of the chilled frosting between two cooled Carrot Cake Cookies to form a sandwich. Assemble the remaining cookies and frosting in the same fashion.

Biscotti with coffee is one of life's little joys. Pick your favorite nut, get baking, and start crunching!

nutty biscotti

BISCOTTI

1¾ cups all-purpose flour

¾ teaspoon baking soda

¼ teaspoon salt

½ cup vegan butter substitute, slightly softened but not at room temperature

¾ cup granulated sugar

2 tablespoons soymilk

1½ teaspoons white vinegar

1 teaspoon vanilla extract

1 teaspoon almond or anise extract or additional vanilla extract

1 teaspoon grated lemon peel

¾ cup finely chopped unsalted nuts

To make the biscotti, preheat the oven to 325 degrees F and oil 3 baking sheets. If you are not using insulated baking sheets, line the baking sheets with parchment paper and spray it with canola oil. Combine the flour, baking soda, and salt in a bowl. In a separate large bowl, combine the vegan butter substitute and sugar and beat with a wooden spoon until smooth. Beat in the soymilk, vinegar, extracts, and lemon peel. Add the flour mixture and stir to combine. Stir in the nuts.

Knead the dough with your hands so that all the flour is incorporated. If the dough feels sticky, add another tablespoon of flour. If the dough is too dry, add a teaspoon or two of soymilk. On a floured surface, form the dough into 2 domed logs, 3 to 4 inches wide and about 2 inches high. Place on 1 of the prepared baking sheets. Bake for about 30 minutes, or until the logs begin to turn light golden brown. Remove from the oven and let cool a few minutes on the baking sheet.

Lower the oven temperature to 275 degrees F. Transfer the logs carefully to a cutting board and cut them with a serrated knife into 1-inch-thick slices (about 12 slices per log). Place the slices cut-side down on the prepared baking sheets and bake for about 12 minutes on each side, until light golden brown. Cool on racks.

Notes

- Good nut choices include pistachios, almonds, walnuts, pine nuts, or macadamia nuts.

- For nut-free biscotti, use vanilla or anise extract and omit the nuts.

GARNISHES *(optional)*

1 cup nondairy chocolate chips

Finely chopped nuts

To make the optional garnish, melt the chocolate chips in a double boiler over gently simmering water. Alternatively, place them in a microwave-safe bowl and microwave at medium power for 1 minute. Stir. Microwave for 25 seconds longer and stir until smooth. If necessary, microwave for an additional 25 seconds. Dip one end of each biscotti into the melted chocolate and then into the chopped nuts, if desired. Place the biscotti on parchment paper to allow the garnish to harden. Store in a sealed container.

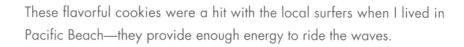

These flavorful cookies were a hit with the local surfers when I lived in Pacific Beach—they provide enough energy to ride the waves.

crunchy peanut butter cookies

1 cup crunchy peanut butter (salted or unsalted)

½ cup vegan butter substitute, slightly softened but not at room temperature

½ cup maple syrup

¼ cup granulated sugar (increase to ⅓ cup if using natural peanut butter)

¼ cup brown sugar

1 teaspoon vanilla extract

2 cups all-purpose flour

½ cup nondairy chocolate chips (optional)

Preheat the oven to 350 degrees F and oil 3 baking sheets. Combine the peanut butter, vegan butter substitute, maple syrup, granulated sugar, brown sugar, and vanilla extract in a bowl and beat with an electric mixer until fluffy. Add the flour and stir until well combined. Stir in the optional chocolate chips.

Form the dough into 1½- to 2-inch balls and arrange them on the prepared baking sheets about 3 inches apart. Use a fork to flatten each cookie and make a crosshatch design, if desired. Bake for about 15 minutes, or until the edges are golden brown. Cool on racks. Store in a sealed container.

Note: If you prefer smoother cookies, use creamy peanut butter instead of crunchy.

Marrying green tea and mint gives these cookies a naturally pretty color. Green tea powder is easy to find at any Asian market. You can also check online retailers and specialty gourmet shops. The flavor of theses cookies is sweet, subtle, and slightly minty. Try serving them with vegan hot chocolate for fun dipping.

minty green tea stars

*NUT FREE   YIELD: ABOUT 60 COOKIES

2 cups all-purpose flour

1 teaspoon baking powder

1 cup granulated sugar

¾ cup vegan butter substitute, slightly softened but not at room temperature

1 tablespoon plus 1 teaspoon peppermint extract

1 tablespoon soy cream cheese

2 ½ teaspoons green tea powder

2 tablespoons soymilk

1 teaspoon vanilla extract

Edible glitter (optional)

Combine the flour and baking powder in a large bowl. In a separate large bowl, combine the sugar, vegan butter substitute, peppermint extract, soy cream cheese, and green tea powder and beat with an electric mixer until fluffy. Add the flour mixture and stir with a wooden spoon to combine. Gather the dough into a ball, cover with plastic wrap, and refrigerate for 2 to 12 hours.

Preheat the oven to 325 degrees F and oil 5 baking sheets. Roll out the dough on a floured surface with a floured rolling pin to about ¼ inch thick. Cut 2-inch stars or other shapes with cookie cutters and arrange on the prepared baking sheets 2 inches apart. Sprinkle with edible glitter, if desired. Bake for 8 to 10 minutes, until the edges barely start to brown. Let the cookies cool on the baking sheets for 2 minutes, then transfer to racks to cool completely. Store in a sealed container.

Vanilla Green Tea Stars:

Replace the peppermint extract with 1 tablespoon of vanilla extract.

These delectable, crescent-shaped cookies are dusted with powdered sugar and will melt in your mouth.

pecan crescents

YIELD: ABOUT 36 COOKIES

1 cup finely chopped toasted pecans

2 cups all-purpose flour

1 teaspoon baking powder

¼ teaspoon salt

1 cup vegan butter substitute, slightly softened but not at room temperature

1½ cups powdered sugar

3 tablespoons soymilk

1 teaspoon vanilla extract

¾ teaspoon almond extract

Preheat the oven to 350 degrees F. Place ½ cup of the pecans in a food processor and pulse until finely ground. Set aside.

Combine the flour, baking powder, and salt in a bowl. In a separate large bowl, combine the vegan butter substitute with ¾ cup of the sugar and beat with an electric mixer until fluffy. Add the flour mixture and the chopped and ground pecans and stir with a wooden spoon to combine. Gather the dough into a ball, cover with plastic wrap, and refrigerate for at least 30 minutes.

Form the dough into 1-inch balls and arrange them on 3 dry baking sheets about 2 inches apart. Flatten and pinch the balls with your fingertips to form crescents. Bake for 15 to 16 minutes, or until they begin to lightly brown. Let the cookies cool for 2 minutes on the baking sheets. Then carefully transfer them to racks and let cool completely.

Put the remaining ¾ cup sugar on a plate and dredge the cooled cookies in it, 1 at a time. Store in a sealed container.

Serve these unique mini-cookie sandwiches for a refreshing treat. Use freshly squeezed orange juice, if possible, for the best taste.

orange burst cookies 'n' cream

*NUT FREE   YIELD: ABOUT 17 COOKIE SANDWICHES

ORANGE BURST COOKIES

2 cups all-purpose flour

1 teaspoon baking powder

½ teaspoon baking soda

⅔ cup vegan butter substitute, slightly softened but not at room temperature

1 cup powdered sugar

2 teaspoons soy cream cheese

⅓ cup orange juice

1 tablespoon plus 1 teaspoon finely grated orange peel

1 teaspoon vanilla extract

⅓ cup candied orange peel, very finely chopped

ORANGE CREAM FILLING

2 ½ cups powdered sugar

½ cup vegan butter substitute, at room temperature

¼ cup soymilk

1 ½ teaspoons vanilla extract

½ teaspoon orange extract

To make the cookies, combine the flour, baking powder, and baking soda in a bowl. In a separate large bowl, combine the vegan butter substitute, sugar, and soy cream cheese and beat with an electric mixer until fluffy. Add the orange juice, orange peel, and vanilla extract and stir with a wooden spoon to combine. Add the flour mixture and candied orange peel and stir to combine. Gather the dough into a ball, cover with plastic wrap, and refrigerate for at least 2 hours or up to 48 hours.

Preheat the oven to 325 degrees F and oil 4 baking sheets. Roll out the dough on a floured surface using a floured rolling pin to ¼ inch thick. Cut the cookies using round cookie cutters (fluted cutters make fancier cookies), about 2½ inches in diameter. Arrange the cookies on the prepared baking sheets about 2 inches apart. Bake for 14 minutes, or until the edges barely begin to brown. The cookies should be light in color but set. Check them often during baking; if the cookies are baking unevenly, turn the baking sheets around. Let the cookies cool on the baking sheets for 2 minutes, then transfer to racks to cool completely.

To make the filling, combine the sugar and vegan butter substitute in a medium bowl and beat with an electric mixer until fluffy. Add the soymilk and extracts and continue to beat until fluffy. Store in a sealed container in the refrigerator for at least 1 hour or up to 24 hours.

To assemble the cookie sandwiches, spread ½ teaspoon of the filling on the flat side of a cooled cookie using a table knife or a pastry bag. Place the flat side of another cookie over the filling. Assemble the remainder of the cookies in the same fashion. Store in a sealed container.

orange burst cookies 'n' cream, page 74

gingerbread guys, page 76

I love the traditional gingerbread form because it is so much fun to make and decorate. Soft and slightly chewy, these cookies can be made crispier if you roll out the dough very thinly. They have broad appeal since they are mildly spiced.

gingerbread guys

*NUT FREE   YIELD: ABOUT 30 COOKIES

GINGERBREAD COOKIES

2 ½ cups all-purpose flour

1 teaspoon baking powder

½ cup vegan butter substitute, slightly softened but not at room temperature

⅓ cup blackstrap or other dark molasses

½ cup maple syrup

¼ cup granulated sugar

1 ½ teaspoons ground ginger

1 teaspoon vanilla extract

1 teaspoon ground cinnamon

¼ teaspoon ground nutmeg

FROSTING

½ cup powdered sugar, sifted

4 teaspoons soymilk

To make the cookies, combine the flour and baking powder in a large bowl. Combine the vegan butter substitute, molasses, maple syrup, and sugar in a separate large bowl and beat with an electric mixer until fluffy. Beat in the ginger, vanilla extract, cinnamon, and nutmeg. Add the flour mixture and stir with a wooden spoon until combined. Gather the dough into a ball, cover with plastic wrap, and refrigerate for 2 to 12 hours.

Preheat the oven to 325 degrees F and oil 5 baking sheets. Roll out the dough on a floured surface with a floured rolling pin to about ¼ inch thick. If necessary, sprinkle additional flour directly on the dough for easier rolling. Cut with 3-inch cookie cutters and arrange on the prepared baking sheets about 2 inches apart. Bake for about 15 minutes, until the cookies are set and slightly puffed. Let the cookies cool on the baking sheets for 3 minutes, then transfer them to racks to cool completely.

To make the frosting, combine the sugar with the soymilk in a small bowl and stir until smooth. Add more soymilk, if necessary, to reach the desired consistency. Pipe designs onto the cooled cookies using a pastry bag or a zipper-lock plastic bag with one of the corners cut off diagonally.

During the holidays, I love giving these hearty cookies as gifts wrapped in beautiful paper. They are wholesome, even with the addition of chocolate.

chocolate-glazed almond cookies

YIELD: ABOUT 24 COOKIES

ALMOND COOKIES

½ cup rolled oats

1 cup raw or lightly toasted sliced or slivered almonds

2 cups all-purpose flour

1 teaspoon baking powder

1 cup vegan butter substitute, slightly softened but not at room temperature

½ cup granulated sugar

1 tablespoon water

1 teaspoon vanilla extract

1 teaspoon almond extract

CHOCOLATE GLAZE

1 cup nondairy chocolate chips

1½ teaspoons vegan butter substitute

1½ teaspoons powdered sugar, sifted

To make the cookies, preheat the oven to 325 degrees F. Grind the oats in a food processor until finely ground but not powdery and set aside.

Grind the almonds in a food processor until finely ground; take care that they do not turn into a paste. Combine the ground oats, ground almonds, flour, and baking powder in a large bowl and set aside.

In a separate large bowl, combine the vegan butter substitute and sugar and beat with a wooden spoon until fluffy. Add the water and extracts and stir to combine. Stir in the flour mixture until just combined. Form into 1-inch balls and arrange them on 3 dry baking sheets about 2 inches apart. Bake for 14 to 16 minutes, until the cookies are set but not brown. Cool on racks.

To make the glaze, melt all the ingredients in a double boiler over gently simmering water. Alternatively, place the ingredients in a microwave-safe bowl and microwave at medium power for 1 minute. Stir. Microwave for 25 seconds longer and stir until smooth. Drizzle the glaze over the cookies with a spoon or pastry bag. Place the cookies on parchment paper until the glaze hardens. Store in a sealed container at room temperature; refrigerate for longer storage.

Plain Almond Cookies: Omit the chocolate glaze and roll the cooled cookies in powdered sugar.

Jam Cookies: Omit the chocolate glaze. Make an indentation in each ball of cookie dough with your finger and fill it with ½ teaspoon of your favorite fruit preserves before baking. For spicier jam cookies, add ½ teaspoon of ground cinnamon and ¼ teaspoon of ground nutmeg to the flour mixture.

Every Saturday night, many years ago, friends and I would go to a kosher bagel store at the Jersey shore to indulge in freshly baked rugalach, bagels, and hot chocolate. It would be awful to have to live without these traditional Jewish roll-up cookies. This vegan version is just as rich as the original. Omit the walnut filling and use only preserves if you want to make this recipe nut free.

rugalach

*CAN BE NUT FREE

YIELD: ABOUT 48 COOKIES

DOUGH

1 cup vegan butter substitute, slightly softened but not at room temperature

1 cup soy cream cheese

1 tablespoon granulated sugar

2 cups all-purpose flour

WALNUT FILLING (optional)

½ cup ground walnuts

¼ cup granulated sugar

1 teaspoon ground cinnamon

FRUIT FILLING

¼ cup fruit preserves of your choice

GARNISH

¼ cup granulated sugar

1 tablespoon ground cinnamon

To make the dough, combine the vegan butter substitute, soy cream cheese, and sugar in a large bowl and beat with an electric mixer until fluffy. Add the flour and mix well with a wooden spoon. Knead the dough into a ball, cover with plastic wrap, and refrigerate for 2 to 12 hours.

To make the optional walnut filling, combine the walnuts, sugar, and cinnamon in a small bowl.

Preheat the oven to 350 degrees F and oil 4 baking sheets. Have ready a small bowl of water.

Divide the chilled dough into 4 equal pieces and work with 1 piece at a time while keeping the others covered and refrigerated. Roll out each piece into a 9-inch disk on a floured surface. Spread a thin layer of fruit preserves over the dough and sprinkle some of the optional walnut filling over it. Cut each disk into 12 wedges using a rolling pizza cutter. Roll up each wedge from the wide end to the narrow point. Dip your fingertips in the bowl of water, wet the edge of the roll, and press to seal. Sprinkle a little sugar and cinnamon on top of each roll.

Arrange the rolls on the prepared baking sheets about 3 inches apart. Bake for 15 minutes, or until the rugalach just begin to lightly brown. Let the rugalach cool on the baking sheets for 2 minutes, then transfer them to racks to cool completely. Store in a sealed container in the refrigerator.

Hamantaschen are small triangular pastries that hold a sweet filling. They are one of the traditional sweets of the Jewish holiday Purim. Here's a vegan version that features a rich, flavorful dough that you can stuff with your favorite filling.

hamantaschen

*NUT FREE   YIELD: ABOUT 36 COOKIES

DOUGH

3 cups all-purpose flour

1 teaspoon baking powder

1/2 teaspoon salt

1 1/4 cups granulated sugar

3/4 cup vegan butter substitute, slightly softened but not at room temperature

1/2 cup soy cream cheese

2 1/2 tablespoons soymilk

1 teaspoon vanilla extract

FILLING

1 cup fruit preserves, or 1 to 2 cans (a total of at least 12.5 ounces) poppy seed, apricot, or date filling

To make the dough, combine the flour, baking powder, and salt in a large bowl. In a separate large bowl, combine the sugar, vegan butter substitute, and soy cream cheese and beat with an electric mixer until fluffy. Beat in the soymilk and vanilla extract. Add the flour mixture and stir with a wooden spoon until just combined. Gather the dough into a ball, cover with plastic wrap, and refrigerate for 2 to 12 hours.

Preheat the oven to 350 degrees F and oil 4 baking sheets. Roll out the dough on a floured surface to barely 1/4 inch thick. Cut into rounds with a 3-inch round cookie cutter to make about 24 rounds.

To fill the hamantaschen, place about 1 teaspoon of filling in the center of each round. Pinch 3 edges of the dough together tightly to prevent the filling from leaking out during baking, leaving the center open, resulting in a triangle shape. Arrange on the prepared baking sheets about 3 inches apart. Bake for 15 to 17 minutes, or until they just begin to brown. Let cool on the baking sheets for 1 minute, then transfer to racks to cool completely. Store in a sealed container in the refrigerator.

Note: If you do not have a three-inch round cookie cutter, you can use the rim of a clean, empty can or drinking glass.

Tiny, adorable, rich, and delicious, these mini-cookie sandwiches taste like the old-style Czech treat my husband grew up munching.

choco-choco sandwich minis

*NUT FREE   YIELD: ABOUT 50 COOKIE SANDWICHES

CHOCOLATE SANDWICH COOKIES

2 cups all-purpose flour

1 teaspoon baking powder

¾ cup vegan butter substitute, slightly softened but not at room temperature

⅔ cup granulated sugar

2 tablespoons soymilk

1 cup nondairy chocolate chips, melted

CHOCOLATE FILLING

¾ cup nondairy chocolate chips

¾ cup vegan butter substitute

2 cups powdered sugar, sifted

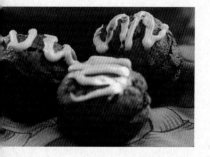

To make the cookies, preheat the oven to 350 degrees F and oil 5 baking sheets. Combine the flour and baking powder in a bowl. In a separate large bowl, combine the vegan butter substitute and sugar and beat with a wooden spoon until creamy. Stir in the soymilk. Add the flour mixture and stir to combine. Add the melted chocolate chips and mix well.

Use a 1-teaspoon measuring spoon as a scoop and arrange scoops of dough, round-side up, on the prepared baking sheets about 2 inches apart. Bake for 7 to 9 minutes, or until the cookies are set but not browned. Let the cookies cool on the baking sheets for 3 minutes, then transfer to racks to cool completely.

To make the filling, melt the chocolate chips and vegan butter substitute in a double boiler over gently simmering water. Alternatively, place them in a microwave-safe bowl and microwave at medium power for 1 minute. Stir. Microwave for 25 seconds longer and stir until smooth. If necessary, microwave for an additional 25 seconds. Stir in the powdered sugar. Beat with an electric mixer or whisk until fluffy and smooth.

To assemble the cookie sandwiches, spread the flat side of a cooled cookie with ½ teaspoon of the filling using a table knife or a pastry bag. Place the flat side of another cookie over the filling. Assemble the remainder of the cookies in the same fashion. Store in a sealed container.

Note: You can make these cookies even tinier by using ½-teaspoon scoops. Or, if you prefer a flatter cookie, roll out the dough and cut it with cookie cutters.

Pair cookies with ice cream and you've got a mini-dessert to chill with or a treat to make a kid's day. Use any of the cookie recipes in *Sweet Utopia* to make ice cream sandwiches your way.

ice cream cookie sandwiches

CAN BE NUT FREE   YIELD: 6 TO 12 COOKIE SANDWICHES

1 recipe cookie dough

1 pint nondairy ice cream

Prepare the cookie dough and preheat the oven according to the recipe directions. Oil 4 baking sheets. Form the dough into 2-inch balls and arrange them on the prepared baking sheets about 4 inches apart. Press down gently on the balls to flatten them slightly.

If the recipe is for rolled cookies, make sure the dough is well chilled. Then roll out the chilled dough and cut it into circles, 3 inches in diameter. The cookies should be slightly thinner than you would normally make them.

Bake according to the recipe directions but add 1 extra minute to the baking time; the cookies should be very lightly browned. Take care not to overbake them, as they should retain some chewiness. Cool on racks.

When cool, freeze the cookies in a single layer, or layer them between parchment paper, for 30 to 60 minutes. To make the cookie sandwiches, place 1 heaping tablespoon of ice cream between the flat side of 2 cookies. Store in sealed plastic containers in the freezer and keep frozen until serving time.

suggested ice cream cookie sandwich combinations

COOKIE DOUGH (CUT ALL INTO CIRCLES)	RECOMMENDED ICE CREAM FLAVORS
Almond Macaroons (page 65)	all flavors
Carrot Cake Cookies (page 67)	vanilla
Choco-Choco Sandwiche Minis (page 80)	all flavors
Chocolate Chippers (page 56)	all flavors except fruity
Crunchy Peanut Butter Cookies (page 71)	vanilla, chocolate, mocha
Fudgy Chip Cookies (page 57)	all flavors
Gingerbread Guys (page 76)	vanilla
Green Speckled Oaties (page 59)	all flavors
Lemon Hearts (page 64)	all flavors except mocha
Minty Green Tea Stars (page 72)	vanilla, chocolate, fruity
Mocha-Almond Chippers (page 58)	all flavors
Orange Burst Cookies 'n' Cream (page 74)	all flavors

Creamy
CHEESECAKES
AND PIES

> *Vegetables are a must on a diet.*
> *I suggest carrot cake, zucchini bread, and pumpkin pie.*
>
> JIM DAVIS, *GARFIELD*

Ever since small cheesecakes were served to athletes at the first Olympic games in 776 BC on the Isle of Delos, people have been enamored of this genre of dessert. But what is a cheesecake without cheese? And how can a pumpkin pie be made without eggs? Brace yourself. This chapter contains some of the most surprisingly creamy, flavorful, nondairy, egg-free, cholesterol-free, guilt-free indulgences you could ever imagine. There are many to choose from, and you can mix and match crusts and fillings for endless variety.

sweet utopia tips

STAY FLEXIBLE

Depending on the size of your family or number of guests, you can make each of the cheesecakes as directed, or turn a cheesecake into a cheesecake pie by cutting the recipe in half and baking it in a pie pan. Conversely, you can turn a cheesecake pie into a cheesecake by doubling the recipe and baking it in a springform pan. A cheesecake pie will take approximately 15 minutes less baking time than a cheesecake.

opposite: luscious lime pie, page 105

SECRETS TO SUCCESS

- For the best taste and texture, prepare cheesecakes 8 to 24 hours in advance.
- If you have a choice of soy cream cheeses, use the one that most closely resembles its dairy counterpart in taste and texture.

Any kind of tofu labeled "silken" will work in the recipes that call for silken tofu.

■ Drain silken tofu well before using it. This is extremely important, especially when you are making vegan cheesecakes, as this step can make or break the texture. Too much fluid will create a ricotta-like texture rather than the desired creamy texture. Drain silken tofu by placing it in a strainer or colander and gently pressing down on it to squeeze out as much extra fluid as you can.

■ Drain soy cream cheese by gently pouring off any extra fluid in the container.

■ Although this might seem unnecessary to mention, make sure you use *plain* (unflavored) soy cream cheese.

■ Do not overblend cheesecake filling; too much air can cause cracking.

BATHING BEAUTIES

■ Using a water bath for cheesecakes makes them creamier. It also protects them from the harsh, direct heat of the oven and helps them to bake more evenly. To create a water bath, place the pan containing the unbaked cheesecake in a larger pan containing a few inches of water (the water should reach three to four inches up the outer sides of the inner pan). Use a water bath for any of the cheesecake recipes in this section.

■ If you are using a springform pan for the cheesecake, wrap the bottom in aluminum foil first to ensure there are no leaks.

IS IT DONE YET?

■ How do you know when a cheesecake is finished baking? The edges will be set and will start to pull away from the sides of the pan. The filling should not be firm, however; if you gently shake the pan, the filling should jiggle a little. It is better to underbake a cheesecake by a few minutes and have it be extra-creamy than to overbake it and have it be tough. When in doubt, take it out!

THE CRUST OF THE MATTER

■ Many store-bought graham cracker and chocolate cookie crusts are vegan and are great to keep in your pantry for when you want to skip a step or need a pie pronto.

- For homemade cookie crusts, look for vegan graham crackers, cookies, tea biscuits, sandwich cookies, and gingersnaps at your local supermarket and natural food store.

- Mix and match crusts for a different take on a cheesecake. The crust recipes in this section make enough for the bottom of a 9-inch springform pan or the bottom and sides of a 9-inch pie pan. To make a crust that goes all the way up the sides of a 9-inch springform pan, double the crust ingredients and follow the instructions as given.

STORAGE

- Cheesecakes and creamy pies should be stored in the refrigerator, loosely covered. Cheesecakes will sweat if they are tightly covered.

- Keep the cheesecake inside the pan until you are ready to serve it. Trying to remove the springform rim before it has thoroughly cooled will cause it to break.

- Keep the cheesecake on the springform plate (bottom) and place it on a larger plate just before serving.

pineapple splash cheesecake, page 94

Any flavor or type of cookie will work for this recipe. Choose one that will complement the filling you are using. You can use this crust with any of the cheesecake recipes in this book, baked or unbaked.

make-your-own crust

30 cookies, 24 tea biscuits, or 18 sandwich cookies

2 tablespoons canola oil

1 tablespoon water

Process the cookies in a food processor or blender until finely ground. Add the oil and water and pulse or stir until combined. Press into a 9-inch pie pan or springform pan and fill.

coconut crust

1 cup rolled oats

½ cup shredded dried coconut (sweetened or unsweetened)

¼ cup canola oil

¼ cup water

3 tablespoons granulated sugar (increase to ¼ cup if using unsweetened coconut)

Preheat the oven to 350 degrees F and oil and flour a 9-inch pie pan or springform pan. Combine the oats and coconut in a food processor or blender and process until coarsely ground. Add the oil, water, and sugar and pulse or stir until combined. Press into the prepared pan. Bake for 12 minutes. Let cool before filling.

Try this crust with any of your favorite cheesecakes, whether they are baked or unbaked.

banana crust

½ cup dried banana chips

1 cup coarsely broken plain or vanilla tea biscuits or graham crackers

2 tablespoons granulated sugar

¼ cup vegan butter substitute, at room temperature

Process the banana chips in a food processor until finely ground. Add the tea biscuits and process until ground. Add the sugar and vegan butter substitute and pulse until combined. Press into a 9-inch pie pan or springform pan and fill.

oat crust

2 cups rolled oats

⅓ cup vegan butter substitute

⅓ cup water

¼ cup granulated sugar

Preheat the oven to 350 degrees F and oil and flour a 9-inch pie pan or springform pan. Process the oats in a food processor or blender until coarsely ground. Add the vegan butter substitute, water, and sugar. Pulse or stir until combined. Press into the prepared pan. Bake for 15 minutes. Let cool before filling.

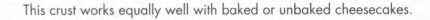

This crust works equally well with baked or unbaked cheesecakes.

chocolate–peanut butter crust

24 chocolate wafer cookies,
18 chocolate tea biscuits, or 12
chocolate sandwich cookies

2 tablespoons creamy peanut
butter (salted or unsalted)

2 tablespoons canola oil

1 tablespoon water

Process the cookies in a food processor or blender until finely ground. Add the peanut butter, oil, and water and pulse or stir until combined. Press into a 9-inch pie pan or springform pan and fill.

date-spelt crust

1 cup spelt flour, whole wheat
flour, or other grain flour of
choice

¼ cup water

2 tablespoons vegan butter
substitute

2 tablespoons granulated,
brown, or turbinado sugar

2 tablespoons very finely
chopped dates

Preheat the oven to 350 degrees F and oil and flour a 9-inch pie pan or springform pan. Combine all the ingredients in a bowl and mix until well combined. Press into the prepared pan. Bake for 12 minutes. Let cool before filling.

graham cracker crust

1½ cups graham cracker pieces or crumbs (about 1 sleeve of graham crackers)

⅓ cup canola oil

1 tablespoon granulated sugar

1 tablespoon water

Preheat the oven to 350 degrees F and oil and flour a 9-inch pie pan or springform pan. Process the graham crackers in a food processor or blender until finely ground. Add the oil, sugar, and water and process until combined. Press into the prepared pan. Bake for 10 minutes. Let cool before filling.

best-ever cherry cheesecake, page 92

This is a "wow" dessert. It never fails to impress and tastes just like any great American cheesecake. No one will believe it's dairy free! I'm a huge fan of canned cherry topping; its sweetness perfectly complements this not-too-sweet confection.

best-ever cherry cheesecake

CRUST

1 Graham Cracker Crust (page 91), prepared in a 9-inch springform pan

FILLING

4 cups soy cream cheese

1 cup granulated sugar

¼ cup lemon juice

2 tablespoons finely ground lemon peel

2 teaspoons cornstarch

2 teaspoons vanilla extract

TOPPING

1 can (21 ounces) cherry pie filling

Preheat the oven to 350 degrees F. Combine the soy cream cheese, sugar, lemon juice, lemon peel, cornstarch, and vanilla extract in a food processor or blender and process until smooth and creamy. Pour into the cooled crust. Bake for 55 minutes, or until the edges are set but the center is not completely firm.

Cool, cover loosely, and refrigerate for 8 to 12 hours before serving. Top with the cherry pie filling just before serving. Store leftovers loosely covered in the refrigerator.

Variations

■ For a twist, substitute lime juice and lime peel for the lemon juice and lemon peel.

■ Try blueberry pie filling, any other fruit pie filling, or fresh fruit as a topping, if you prefer.

Silky citrus is married with wild berries in this classic cheesecake pie recipe. It can be served plain or dressed up with Strawberry Sauce. Serve it for an Independence Day celebration topped with fresh blueberries instead of strawberries for a spectacular red, white, and blue delight.

fresh strawberry cheesecake pie

*NUT FREE

YIELD: 8 SERVINGS

CRUST

1 Graham Cracker Crust (page 91), prepared in a 9-inch pie pan

FILLING

1½ cups firm silken tofu, well drained

1 cup soy cream cheese

1 cup granulated sugar

2 tablespoons lemon and/or lime juice

1 tablespoon finely ground lemon and/or lime peel

1 teaspoon cornstarch

1 teaspoon vanilla extract

STRAWBERRY SAUCE

½ cup fresh or frozen strawberries

¼ cup granulated sugar

½ cup water

1½ teaspoons cornstarch

GARNISH *(optional)*

2 to 3 cups fresh strawberries

To make the cheesecake, preheat the oven to 350 degrees F. Combine the tofu, soy cream cheese, sugar, juice, peel, cornstarch, and vanilla extract in a food processor or blender and process until smooth and creamy. Bake for 55 minutes, or until the edges are set but the center is not completely firm. Cool, cover loosely, and refrigerate for 8 to 12 hours before serving.

To make the sauce, combine all the ingredients in a food processor or blender and process until almost smooth. Push through a fine-mesh strainer. Transfer to a small saucepan and cook on medium heat, stirring often, just until the sauce begins to bubble, about 5 minutes.

To make the optional garnish, cut the stems and bottoms off the strawberries and arrange them tip-side up on top of the cake just before serving.

To serve, pour the Strawberry Sauce over individual slices or drizzle the sauce on the side of the plate. Garnish with additional strawberries, if desired. Store leftovers loosely covered in the refrigerator.

Strawberry Cheesecake: Prepare the crust in a 9-inch springform pan. Double the filling ingredients but use only 1⅔ cups sugar. Bake for 1 hour and 10 minutes.

Raspberry Cheesecake Pie: Replace the strawberries in the sauce and garnish with an equal amount of raspberries.

Mixed-Berry Cheesecake Pie: Replace the strawberries in the sauce with an equal amount of mixed berries. Garnish with any berries you like.

This tropical takeoff on the classic cheesecake is a breeze to prepare. To maintain a rich, creamy texture, I use only dried pineapple in this recipe. The dried pineapple absorbs excess moisture, which plumps it up during baking.

pineapple splash cheesecake

*NUT FREE

YIELD: 12 SERVINGS

CRUST

1 Graham Cracker Crust (page 91), **prepared in a 9-inch springform pan**

FILLING

3 cups firm silken tofu, well drained

2 cups soy cream cheese

1¼ cups granulated sugar

2 teaspoons cornstarch

2 teaspoons lemon juice

2 teaspoons vanilla extract

¼ cup finely chopped dried or candied pineapple

GLAZED PINEAPPLE TOPPING

1 can (20 ounces) pineapple rings packed in juice, drained (reserve juice)

2 cups pineapple juice (include the reserved juice from the pineapple)

¾ cup granulated sugar

¼ cup light corn syrup

To make the filling, preheat the oven to 350 degrees F. Combine the tofu, soy cream cheese, sugar, cornstarch, lemon juice, and vanilla extract in a food processor or blender and process until smooth and creamy. Stir in the dried pineapple. Pour into the cooled crust. Bake for 1 hour and 10 minutes, or until the edges are set but the center is not completely firm. Cool, cover loosely, and refrigerate for 8 to 12 hours before serving.

To make the topping, squeeze out any excess liquid from the pineapple rings and pat them dry with a paper towel. Combine the pineapple juice, sugar, and corn syrup in a medium saucepan. Bring to a boil on medium heat and cook, stirring often, for about 10 minutes. Add the pineapple rings and simmer, stirring occasionally, until they are almost translucent and the liquid is greatly reduced, 25 to 30 minutes. Stir carefully so the rings hold their shape. Remove the pineapple rings from the liquid and place them on racks for 8 to 12 hours at room temperature, or until completely dry. Store them in a sealed plastic container in the refrigerator for up to 7 days.

Top the cheesecake with the glazed pineapple just before serving. Store leftover cheesecake loosely covered in the refrigerator.

Variation: For a dramatic color contrast, drizzle Strawberry Sauce (page 93) over each slice just before serving.

Inspired by the classic Japanese green tea cake, this beautiful cheesecake is a work of art when you whirl together the green and white batters. It's the only cheesecake that captures my favorite color naturally. You can find green tea powder at Asian markets or gourmet shops, or you can order it through online retailers. What a delicious way to get your antioxidants!

green tea swirl cheesecake

*NUT FREE   YIELD: 12 SERVINGS

CRUST

1 Oat Crust (page 89) or other crust of your choice, prepared in a 9-inch springform pan

FILLING

3 cups firm silken tofu, well drained

3 cups soy cream cheese

1⅓ cups plus 1 tablespoon granulated sugar

2 teaspoons cornstarch

2 teaspoons vanilla extract

1 teaspoon lemon juice

1 tablespoon plus ½ teaspoon green tea powder

1 tablespoon orange juice

1 tablespoon finely grated orange peel

2 to 3 drops green food coloring (optional)

Preheat the oven to 350 degrees F. Combine the tofu, soy cream cheese, 1⅓ cups of the sugar, and all of the cornstarch, vanilla extract, and lemon juice in a blender or food processor and process until smooth and creamy.

Transfer ¾ cup of the blended mixture to a small bowl and add the green tea powder, orange juice, orange peel, remaining tablespoon of sugar, and the optional food coloring.

Pour the white blended mixture into the cooled crust. Place dollops of the green tea mixture evenly over the top of the white mixture. Run a knife zigzag through the batter to create a marble effect (take care not to blend the two mixtures or the marble effect will be lost). Bake for 1 hour and 10 minutes, or until the edges are set but the center is not completely firm. Cool, cover loosely, and refrigerate for 8 to 12 hours before serving.

Minted Green Tea Cheesecake: Omit the orange juice and orange peel. Add 1 tablespoon of peppermint extract to the green tea mixture. For extra-minty cheesecake, also add 1 tablespoon of peppermint extract to the tofu mixture prior to blending. This variation tastes great with Make-Your-Own Crust (page 88) made with chocolate cookies.

Green Tea Swirl Cheesecake Pie: Cut the filling recipe in half. Use a pie pan and bake for 50 minutes.

coconut-almond cheesecake pie, page 97

Here's an enchanting combination. Coconut and almond flavors play off each other in this ultra-creamy, no-bake pie. It's the ultimate treat for a summer dinner outdoors. Use a premade vegan pie crust if you want to make a delectable dessert in ten minutes.

coconut-almond cheesecake pie

*NO BAKE   YIELD: 8 SERVINGS

CRUST

1 Coconut Crust (page 88) or Graham Cracker Crust (page 91), prepared in a 9-inch pie pan

FILLING

1½ cups firm silken tofu, well drained

1 cup soy cream cheese

1 cup granulated sugar

1 tablespoon plus ½ teaspoon coconut extract

½ teaspoon almond extract

½ cup full-fat coconut milk

¼ cup cornstarch

GARNISH

½ cup shredded dried coconut (sweetened or unsweetened), toasted

½ cup toasted sliced or slivered almonds

Combine the tofu, soy cream cheese, sugar, and extracts in a food processor or blender and process until smooth and creamy. Do not remove from the food processor or blender.

Combine the coconut milk and cornstarch in a small saucepan and stir with a whisk until smooth. Cook on medium heat, whisking often, for about 3 minutes, or until thickened and smooth. Immediately remove from the heat and add to the tofu mixture. Process again until smooth and creamy.

Pour into the cooled crust and garnish with the coconut and almonds. Cover loosely and refrigerate for 8 to 12 hours before serving. Store leftovers loosely covered in the refrigerator.

This creamy variation of pumpkin pie is a delightful change of pace during the holidays.

pumpkin cheesecake pie

CRUST

1 Graham Cracker Crust (page 91), prepared in a 9-inch pie pan

FILLING

1½ cups silken tofu, well drained

1 cup soy cream cheese

1 cup canned pumpkin

1 cup granulated sugar

2 teaspoons ground cinnamon

1 teaspoon cornstarch

1 teaspoon ground ginger

1 teaspoon ground nutmeg

Preheat the oven to 350 degrees F. Combine all the filling ingredients in a food processor or blender and process until smooth and creamy. Pour into the cooled crust. Bake for 55 minutes, or until lightly browned and the edges are set. Cool, cover loosely, and refrigerate for 8 to 12 hours before serving. Store leftovers loosely covered in the refrigerator.

Rejoice! This rich, creamy cheesecake has a secret surprise—
the tantalizing taste of almonds.

almond cheesecake pie

YIELD: 8 SERVINGS

CRUST

1 Graham Cracker Crust
(page 91), **prepared in a
9-inch pie pan**

FILLING

1 package (15 ounces) **firm
or extra-firm regular tofu,
well drained and patted dry**

1 cup soy cream cheese

1 cup minus 2 tablespoons
granulated sugar

1 tablespoon almond butter
(see note)

1 teaspoon lemon juice

1 teaspoon vanilla extract

¾ teaspoon almond extract

Preheat the oven to 350 degrees F. Combine all the filling ingredients in a food processor or blender and process until smooth and creamy. Pour into the cooled crust. Bake for 1 hour, or until lightly browned and the edges are set. Cool, cover loosely, and refrigerate for 8 to 12 hours before serving. Store leftovers loosely covered in the refrigerator.

Note: If you don't have almond butter, process ¼ cup of almonds in a blender or food processor until very finely ground. Add the lemon juice to the almonds to facilitate processing, if desired.

Almond Cheesecake: Prepare the Graham Cracker Crust in a 9-inch springform pan. Double the filling recipe and add 2 teaspoons of cornstarch. Bake for 1 hour and 10 minutes, or until the edges are set but the center is not completely firm.

Chocolate lovers will gasp with joy after biting into this insanely rich cheesecake pie. Serve it plain or with Nutty Crème (page 132) or Coconut Crème (page 133).

chocolate cheesecake pie

*NUT FREE   YIELD: 8 SERVINGS

CRUST

1 Make-Your-Own Crust (page 88) **made with chocolate cookies, prepared in a 9-inch pie pan**

FILLING

1½ cups firm silken tofu, well drained

1 cup soy cream cheese

1 cup nondairy chocolate chips, melted

1 cup minus 2 tablespoons granulated sugar

3 tablespoons unsweetened cocoa powder

1 teaspoon cornstarch

1 teaspoon vanilla extract

Preheat the oven to 350 degrees F. Combine all the filling ingredients in a food processor or blender and process until smooth and creamy. Pour into the cooled crust. Bake for 55 minutes, or until the edges are set. Cool, cover loosely, and refrigerate for 8 to 12 hours before serving. Store leftovers loosely covered in the refrigerator.

Chocolate Cheesecake: Prepare the crust in a 9-inch springform pan and double the filling recipe. Bake for 1 hour and 10 minutes, or until the edges are set but the center is not completely firm.

Note: For some texture in the cheesecake filling, don't melt some or all of the chocolate chips. Process them with the other filling ingredients until they are coarsely ground.

These portable little cakes are so much fun, especially for kids and parties.

peanut butter mini-cheesecakes

CRUST

1 recipe Chocolate–Peanut Butter Crust (page 90)

FILLING

1½ cups firm silken tofu, well drained

1 cup soy cream cheese

1 cup creamy peanut butter (salted or unsalted)

1 cup granulated sugar (plus 2 tablespoons if using natural peanut butter)

1 teaspoon cornstarch

1 teaspoon vanilla extract

CHOCOLATE GLAZE

⅓ cup nondairy chocolate chips

2 tablespoons vegan butter substitute

2 tablespoons granulated sugar

½ teaspoon vanilla extract

GARNISH (optional)

2 tablespoons chopped unsalted roasted peanuts

To make the crust, line a 12-cup standard muffin pan with foil or paper liners. Press the crust mixture evenly into each cup.

To make the filling, preheat the oven to 350 degrees F. Combine all the filling ingredients in a food processor or blender and process until smooth and creamy. Spoon into the crust-lined muffin cups until heaping. Bake for 20 minutes, or until lightly browned and the edges are set. Cool the cheesecakes in the pan, then refrigerate them in the pan for 4 to 12 hours before serving.

To make the glaze, melt the chocolate chips, vegan butter substitute, and sugar in a double boiler over gently simmering water. Alter-

natively, combine them in a microwave-safe bowl and microwave at medium power for 1 minute. Stir. Microwave for 25 seconds longer and stir until smooth. If necessary, microwave for an additional 25 seconds. Stir in the vanilla extract.

Just before serving, remove the cheesecakes from the pan, peel off the liners, arrange on individual serving plates, and spoon the glaze on top. Garnish with the optional peanuts, if desired. Store leftover mini-cheesecakes in a sealed container in the refrigerator.

Layers are fun, and with this recipe you get all your favorite cheesecake flavors layered into a handy, portable bar. Although there are a few steps involved, they are quick and easy.

three-layer cheesecake bars

*NUT FREE   **YIELD: 24 BARS**

CRUST

2 Make-Your-Own Crust (page 88) made with chocolate cookies

BASE FILLING

3 cups firm silken tofu, well drained

2 cups soy cream cheese

1¾ cups granulated sugar

2 tablespoons all-purpose flour

1 tablespoon cornstarch

2 teaspoons vanilla extract

VANILLA LAYER

1 teaspoon vanilla extract

1 teaspoon lemon juice

CHOCOLATE LAYER

⅔ cup nondairy chocolate chips, melted

¼ cup unsweetened cocoa powder

COCONUT LAYER

⅔ cup shredded dried coconut (sweetened or unsweetened)

1 teaspoon coconut extract

To make the crust, preheat the oven to 350 degrees F and line a 9 x 13-inch baking pan with aluminum foil (the foil should extend over the sides of the pan). Oil the bottom and sides of the foil. Press the crust mixture into the bottom of the pan and ¼ inch up the sides.

To make the base filling, combine all the base recipe ingredients in a food processor or blender and process until smooth and creamy. Divide the mixture evenly among 3 bowls.

To make the vanilla layer, whisk the vanilla extract and lemon juice into the first bowl of the base filling.

To make the chocolate layer, transfer the second bowl of the base filling to a food processor or blender. Add the melted chocolate chips and cocoa powder and process until smooth.

To make the coconut layer, whisk the coconut and coconut extract into the third bowl of the base filling.

Pour the vanilla layer into the crust and spread it out evenly. Place dollops of the chocolate layer over the vanilla layer and spread it out evenly. Place dollops of the coconut layer over the chocolate layer and spread it out evenly. Bake for 50 minutes, or until the edges are set but the center is not completely firm. Cool, cover loosely, and refrigerate for 8 to 12 hours before serving. Store leftovers loosely covered in the refrigerator.

Vanilla-Chocolate-Peanut Butter Bars: Omit the coconut and coconut extract. Whisk ½ cup of peanut butter into the third bowl of base filling.

Vanilla-Lemon-Coconut Bars: Omit the chocolate chips and cocoa powder. Whisk 2 tablespoons of lemon juice, 1 tablespoons of grated lemon peel, and 2 teaspoons of lemon extract into the second bowl of base filling.

three-layer cheesecake bars, page 102

mocha-marble cheesecake, page 104

A ribbon of mocha zigzags throughout this ultra-creamy cheesecake and adds a touch of sophistication to an otherwise simple dessert. It looks fancy but is so easy to make. Although a water bath is optional for most cheesecake recipes, it is essential for this one to obtain the creamy texture.

mocha-marble cheesecake

*NUT FREE   YIELD: 12 SERVINGS

CRUST

1 Make-Your-Own Crust (page 88) made with chocolate sandwich cookies, prepared in a 9-inch springform pan

FILLING

3 cups firm silken tofu, well drained

2 cups soy cream cheese

1¼ cups granulated sugar

2 teaspoons vanilla extract

2 teaspoons cornstarch

1½ teaspoons lemon juice

¼ cup chocolate chips, melted

2 teaspoons instant espresso powder or granules

Preheat the oven to 350 degrees F. Wrap the bottom of the springform pan containing the crust with aluminum foil and prepare a water bath (see page 86).

Combine the tofu, soy cream cheese, sugar, vanilla extract, cornstarch, and lemon juice in a food processor or blender and process until smooth and creamy. Set aside ½ cup of the tofu mixture and pour the remainder into the prepared crust.

Add the melted chocolate chips and espresso powder to the reserved tofu mixture. Stir until completely smooth. Place dollops of the chocolate mixture evenly over the white batter in the pan. Run a knife zigzag through the batter to create a marble effect (take care not to blend the two mixtures or the marble effect will be lost).

Place in the water bath and bake for 1 hour and 10 minutes, or until the edges are set but the center is not completely firm. Cool, cover loosely, and refrigerate for 8 to 12 hours before serving. Store leftovers loosely covered in the refrigerator.

Mint-Chocolate Swirl Cheesecake: Omit the lemon juice and espresso powder. Add 2 tablespoons of peppermint extract to the tofu mixture before blending.

Mocha-Marble Cheesecake Pie: Prepare the crust in a 9-inch pie pan. Cut the ingredients in half and bake for 55 minutes, or until lightly browned and the edges are set. You will still need to use a water bath.

Cool and tangy, this pie is a creamy and delightful version of key lime pie—a real hit! It doesn't get very firm, but the loose, soft filling is soothing and refreshing. Serve plain or with Lemon Crème (page 133) or Coconut Crème (page 133).

luscious lime pie

CRUST

1 Graham Cracker Crust (page 91), prepared in a 9-inch pie pan

FILLING

1½ cups firm silken tofu, well drained

1 cup soy cream cheese

1 cup granulated sugar

¼ cup plus 1 tablespoon cornstarch

½ cup lime juice (about 2 large limes)

2 tablespoons finely grated lime peel

2 teaspoons vanilla extract

Combine the tofu and soy cream cheese in a food processor or blender and process until smooth and creamy. Combine the sugar and cornstarch in a small bowl, mix well, and add to the tofu mixture. Process again, stopping to scrape down the sides of the container as needed, until completely smooth.

Transfer to a medium saucepan and cook on medium heat, stirring almost constantly, for 5 to 7 minutes, or until the mixture begins to thicken. It should not come to a boil or begin to get lumpy. Pour into a bowl and stir in the lime juice, lime peel, and vanilla extract. Stir constantly until well combined, mashing any small lumps that may have formed. Pour into the cooled crust. Cool, cover loosely, and refrigerate for 8 to 12 hours before serving. Store leftovers loosely covered in the refrigerator.

This pie is the pièce de résistance. It looks like a thick brownie pie but with plenty more toasted pecans. Melted chocolate oozes from each liqueur-laced slice, while the crisp nuts set off the rich, chewy filling. Although it's captivating, irresistible, and unique, you won't believe how easy it is to make. Serve it plain or with Nutty Crème (page 132), vanilla soy ice cream, or a tall glass of soymilk.

chocolate-pecan paradise pie

YIELD: 8 SERVINGS

CRUST

1 Graham Cracker Crust (page 91), prepared in a 9-inch pie pan

FILLING

½ cup rolled oats

⅓ cup all-purpose flour

½ teaspoon salt

⅔ cup warm vanilla soymilk

½ cup maple syrup

¼ cup vegan butter substitute, at room temperature

3 tablespoons blackstrap or other dark molasses

2 tablespoons liqueur (such as amaretto, chocolate, coffee, hazelnut, or rum) **or** flavored syrup for coffee

2 cups chopped lightly toasted pecans

1 cup nondairy chocolate chips

Preheat the oven to 350 degrees F. Process the oats in a blender or food processor until they are very finely ground but not powdery. Transfer to a bowl and stir in the flour and salt.

In a separate large bowl, combine the soymilk, maple syrup, vegan butter substitute, molasses, and liqueur and whisk until smooth. Whisk in the flour mixture. Stir in the pecans and chocolate chips with a wooden spoon. Pour into the cooled crust. Bake for 38 to 40 minutes, or until the filling is set.

Serve warm. Store leftovers tightly covered in the refrigerator.

Walnut or Mixed-Nut Pie: Replace all or some of the pecans with chopped lightly toasted walnuts.

Notes

■ To freshen leftovers, warm slices in the microwave for up to 1 minute on medium power just before serving.

■ For a more brownielike filling, melt the chocolate chips and add them to the soymilk mixture.

■ If you do not have vanilla soymilk, use ⅔ cup of plain sweetened soymilk plus ¼ teaspoon of vanilla extract.

Lemon and berries are such a fanciful combination and the colors are eye-popping. This light and refreshing yet simple tart is perfect for the summer. Serve it plain or with Lemon Crème (page 133) or Coconut Crème (page 133). This is also wonderfully refreshing prepared in mini tart pans and served frozen.

lemon-berry tart

*NUT FREE   YIELD: 8 SERVINGS

CRUST

1 Graham Cracker Crust (page 91), prepared in a 9-inch tart or pie pan

LEMON FILLING

¼ cup cornstarch

2 cups vanilla soymilk

⅔ cup granulated sugar

¼ cup plus 2 tablespoons lemon juice

1½ tablespoons finely grated lemon peel

1½ teaspoons lemon extract

1 teaspoon vanilla extract

GARNISH

2 to 3 cups sliced strawberries, raspberries, and/or blackberries

To make the filling, combine the cornstarch with 3 to 4 tablespoons of the soymilk in a medium saucepan and whisk until there are no lumps. Place on medium heat and whisk in the remainder of the soymilk and all of the sugar. Cook, whisking often, for about 7 minutes, or until the mixture thickens but does not boil. Whisk vigorously as it thickens so that the mixture is smooth. Remove from heat and pour into a medium bowl. Immediately whisk in the lemon juice, lemon peel, and extracts. Whisk rapidly until the mixture is smooth with no lumps. Pour into the cooled crust. Cool, cover loosely, and refrigerate for 3 to 5 hours before serving.

To garnish, top with the strawberries arranged in a spiral just before serving. Store leftovers loosely covered in the refrigerator.

Spicy and heartier than traditional pumpkin pie, this is easy to make and a real crowd pleaser during the holidays.

pumpkin-nut pie

YIELD: 8 SERVINGS

CRUST

1 Graham Cracker Crust (page 91), prepared in a 9-inch pie pan

PUMPKIN FILLING

1½ cups silken tofu, well drained

1 cup canned pumpkin

1 cup granulated sugar

2 teaspoons cornstarch

1 teaspoon vanilla extract

1 teaspoon ground nutmeg

1 teaspoon ground cinnamon

¼ teaspoon ground cloves (optional)

WALNUT TOPPING

⅓ cup chopped walnuts

2 tablespoons brown sugar

1½ tablespoons vegan butter substitute, at room temperature

1 teaspoon ground cinnamon

To make the filling, preheat the oven to 350 degrees F. Combine all the filling ingredients in a food processor or blender and process until very smooth and creamy. Pour into the cooled crust. Bake for 40 minutes.

To make the topping, combine all the ingredients in a small bowl.

After the pie has baked for 40 minutes, remove it from the oven and immediately sprinkle the topping evenly over the top. Return the pie to the oven and bake for 20 minutes longer, or until the topping is golden brown and the filling is set. Cool, cover loosely, and refrigerate for 4 to 8 hours before serving. Bring to room temperature before serving. Store leftovers loosely covered in the refrigerator.

Velvety
MOUSSES PUDDINGS AND CREMES

> *Never spare the Parson's wine,*
> *nor the Baker's pudding.*
>
> BENJAMIN FRANKLIN, *POOR RICHARD'S ALMANAC*

Just because you don't eat dairy products doesn't mean you need to skimp on pudding! Soothe your soul and indulge your sweet tooth with these creamy custards, mousses, and crèmes. Some are rich and warming, while others are unexpectedly fruity, refreshing, and zesty.

sweet utopia tips

GET ADVENTUROUS

- Many of the recipes in this section call for soymilk. Because it is the thickest nondairy milk alternative, it makes the richest-tasting puddings. However, you can substitute any other kind of nondairy milk you like for the soymilk—try almond, cashew, hazelnut, hemp, oat, sesame, or rice milk.

- When using these alternatives to soymilk, also add a little coconut milk to contribute more richness. It should constitute one-third to one-half of the total nondairy milk called for in the recipe.

HOW SWEET IT IS

- If no particular type of soymilk is specified, use plain or vanilla sweetened soymilk. If you use unsweetened soymilk, increase the sugar in the recipe to taste.

opposite: layered cream gels with fruit, page 125

- Some of the recipes in this section call for granulated sugar, while others call for turbinado. Turbinado or raw sugar will give these recipes a rich, earthy taste.

SECRETS TO SUCCESS

- Any kind of tofu labeled "silken" will work in the recipes that call for silken tofu.
- Use any thickener you like. Although I call for cornstarch in the recipes, because it is the easiest to obtain and the least expensive, arrowroot and kuzu starch also work well in these recipes. Substitute them measure for measure for the cornstarch.
- Keep pudding smooth while it is cooking by whisking it often; however, do not whisk so vigorously that air is incorporated or bubbles or foam are created.
- Always use a heavy-bottomed saucepan (not a skillet) for puddings and custards that are cooked on the stovetop.
- Maintain moderate heat. If the heat is too high, the pudding will scorch and be ruined.

STORAGE

- Press plastic wrap onto the surface of warm pudding to prevent a skin from forming. If you prefer skin on the pudding, keep the pudding uncovered until it has cooled, then cover it tightly with plastic wrap and refrigerate.
- Mousses, tapioca, and rice pudding won't form a skin. Cool them at room temperature, then cover them tightly with plastic wrap and refrigerate.

DRESS IT UP

- Dress up a pudding or mousse with dollops of your favorite vegan crème (see pages 132–133) or vegan whipped cream.
- Serve puddings in a beautiful glass or bowl for a sophisticated presentation.

pudding parfait, page 130

The first time I read the ingredients on an instant pudding box, I knew I never wanted to serve it to my family. Now you don't have to either! Rekindle your childhood memories with this basic yet fantastic pudding. Any connoisseur will appreciate its velvety texture and rich chocolate taste. Serve it plain or with your choice of crème (see pages 132–133) and/or fresh berries.

divine chocolate pudding

*NUT FREE   YIELD: 6 SERVINGS

¼ cup unsweetened cocoa powder

⅓ cup granulated sugar

2 tablespoons cornstarch

¼ teaspoon salt

2 cups vanilla soymilk

1 teaspoon vanilla extract

½ teaspoon almond extract or additional vanilla extract

⅓ cup nondairy chocolate chips

Sift the cocoa powder into a medium saucepan. Mix in the sugar, cornstarch, and salt until there are no lumps. Place on low to medium heat and slowly whisk in the soymilk until the mixture is smooth. Cook on medium heat, whisking constantly, for about 10 minutes, or until thickened (it should be the consistency of cake batter). Do not let the mixture come to a boil. Remove from the heat and stir in the extracts. Then stir in the chocolate chips and continue stirring until they are completely melted.

Pour evenly into six 6-ounce ramekins or a large bowl. Cool, cover tightly with plastic wrap, and refrigerate for 4 to 8 hours before serving, or until thoroughly chilled. Store leftover pudding tightly covered in the refrigerator.

Here's a recipe for the almond lover in you. It is scrumptious yet unusual and is very hearty and rich. It works great layered in parfaits, served with cookies, or topped with your choice of crème.

almond pudding

YIELD: 4 SERVINGS

¼ cup cornstarch

2 cups vanilla almond milk

¼ cup plus 2 tablespoons turbinado sugar

2 tablespoons unsalted creamy almond butter

½ teaspoon almond extract

Place the cornstarch in a small saucepan on medium heat. Whisk in 3 to 4 tablespoons of the almond milk and continue whisking for 2 to 4 minutes, until there are no lumps. Do not let the mixture come to a boil.

Whisk in the remaining almond milk and all of the sugar, almond butter, and almond extract. Continue to cook on medium heat, whisking often, until the mixture thickens but does not boil, about 8 minutes.

Pour evenly into four 6-ounce ramekins. Cool, cover tightly with plastic wrap, and refrigerate for 4 to 8 hours before serving. Store leftover pudding tightly covered in the refrigerator.

I loved the homemade vegetarian meals the Hare Krishnas served us at my university in San Diego. But traditional Indian desserts are loaded with ghee (clarified butter) and cream. The perfect blend of sweetness and spice in this carrot-based dessert hits the spot after a curry dinner. It's a great way to enjoy your veggies!

carrot-ginger pudding

CARROT-GINGER PUDDING

¼ cup cornstarch

2 cups vanilla soymilk or almond milk

2 jars (3.5 to 4 ounces per jar) carrot baby food, or ½ cup plus 1 tablespoon puréed cooked carrots

½ cup turbinado sugar

3 tablespoons finely chopped crystallized or candied ginger

1 teaspoon vanilla extract

½ teaspoon ground cardamom

GARNISH (optional)

¼ cup finely chopped pistachios and/or raisins

Place the cornstarch in a small saucepan on medium heat. Whisk in 3 to 4 tablespoons of the soymilk and continue whisking for 2 to 4 minutes, until there are no lumps. Do not let the mixture come to a boil.

Add the remaining soymilk and all of the carrot baby food, sugar, ginger, vanilla extract, and cardamom and cook, whisking often, until the mixture thickens but does not boil, about 10 minutes. Pour evenly into six 6-ounce ramekins. Cool, cover tightly with plastic wrap, and refrigerate for 4 to 8 hours before serving.

Garnish with the pistachios and/or raisins just before serving, if desired. Store leftover pudding tightly covered in the refrigerator.

There's nothing in the world like a mango straight from the tree. I had the pleasure of feasting on the iridescent orange flesh of tree-ripened mangoes that fell to the ground in my grandmother's backyard in Israel. The flavors of super-fresh mango and lime make this pudding a great summer treat.

mango-lime pudding

*NUT FREE   YIELD: 6 SERVINGS

2 cups fresh or thawed frozen mango chunks

1 cup soymilk

⅓ cup granulated sugar

¼ cup lime juice

3 tablespoons agar powder

Combine the mango, soymilk, sugar, lime juice, and agar powder in a food processor or blender and process until smooth. Transfer to a medium saucepan and cook on medium heat, stirring often, until it reaches a boil, about 5 minutes. Remove from the heat and mix until completely smooth and there are no lumps.

Pour evenly into six 6-ounce ramekins. Cool, cover tightly with plastic wrap, and refrigerate for 4 to 8 hours before serving. Store leftover pudding tightly covered in the refrigerator.

Note: A small amount of agar powder is used in the recipe. Agar is a sea vegetable with natural gelling properties. It does not make the pudding firm (like animal-based gelatin would), but it helps hold the pudding together and gives it body. You can purchase agar powder at Asian markets and natural food stores or from online retailers.

Why miss out on creamy rice pudding just because you don't use dairy products? Unexpectedly rich, this is a satisfying version of this classic dessert.

rice pudding

YIELD: 6 SERVINGS

RICE

¾ cup white basmati rice, unrinsed

2 cups water

CREAM

1½ cups silken tofu, well drained

¾ cup granulated sugar

1 teaspoon vanilla extract

1 teaspoon ground cinnamon

½ teaspoon almond extract or additional vanilla extract

GARNISH (optional)

Toasted slivered almonds

Ground cinnamon

To make the rice, combine the rice and water in a medium saucepan. Cover and cook on medium heat for about 15 minutes. Remove from the heat and let rest for about 10 minutes, covered, until the water is absorbed.

To make the cream, combine all the ingredients in a blender or food processor and process until smooth. Fold into the cooked rice in the saucepan.

Spoon evenly into six 6-ounce ramekins. Cool, cover tightly with plastic wrap, and refrigerate for 4 to 8 hours before serving. Garnish with almonds and cinnamon just before serving, if desired. Store leftover pudding tightly covered in the refrigerator.

This dessert so perfectly captures the taste of the islands, I can almost feel the ocean breeze whenever I make it. I buy the best Thai coconut milk in cans from an Asian market; it imparts such a decadent taste and is the secret touch that makes this vegan tapioca pudding so rich.

coconut tapioca pudding

*NUT FREE   YIELD: 4 SERVINGS

PUDDING

⅓ cup quick-cooking tapioca

1 cup water

1 can (14 ounces) full-fat coconut milk

½ cup turbinado sugar

⅛ teaspoon salt

FRUIT TOPPING

1 cup fresh or frozen berries and/or diced mango or other fruit of choice

⅓ cup granulated sugar or agave syrup

To make the pudding, combine the tapioca and water in a medium saucepan and let soak at room temperature for 20 to 25 minutes. Most of the water will be absorbed, and the tapioca should be soft but not stuck together. Add the coconut milk, sugar, and salt. Cook on low heat for 7 to 9 minutes, stirring often with a wooden spoon, until the mixture thickens. Do not let the mixture come to a boil.

Spoon evenly into four 6-ounce ramekins. Cool, cover tightly with plastic wrap, and refrigerate for 4 to 8 hours before serving. Store leftover pudding tightly covered in the refrigerator.

To make the topping, combine the fruit and the sugar in a blender or food processor and process until almost smooth. Spoon over the pudding just before serving. Store leftover topping in a sealed container in the refrigerator.

Notes

■ This pudding is great with chocolate syrup instead of or in addition to the fruit topping.

■ The fruit topping can be made one day in advance and stored in a sealed container in the refrigerator.

My mother, who was always an avid entertainer, was famous for serving the richest chocolate mousse in town. I went without it for many years because it is traditionally made with eggs and cream. I finally created my own version of this super-rich mousse, and it's exactly what a chocolate lover wants! The liqueur gives it a distinctive, adult flavor.

chocolate mousse

*NUT FREE   YIELD: 4 SERVINGS

1½ cups silken tofu, at room temperature, well drained

1 cup nondairy chocolate chips, melted

½ cup granulated sugar

2 to 3 tablespoons rum or other liqueur (such as amaretto, coffee, or hazelnut) or a combination, or 2 tablespoons water

1 teaspoon vanilla extract

1 teaspoon instant coffee granules (optional)

Combine all the ingredients in a food processor or blender. Process until smooth and creamy. Spoon evenly into four 6-ounce ramekins. Cover tightly with plastic wrap and refrigerate for 4 to 8 hours before serving. Store leftover mousse tightly covered in the refrigerator.

Chocolate Mousse Pie: Spoon the mousse into the pie crust of your choice. Refrigerate for 6 to 12 hours. If desired, garnish with toasted nuts and Nutty Crème (page 132) or the crème of your choice.

Chocolate-Orange Mousse: Omit the coffee and add 1 tablespoon of finely grated orange peel and ½ teaspoon of orange extract.

cappuccino custard, page 121

This custard has a multidimensional taste that appeals to adults. The starch, in combination with a high-quality soymilk, gives this custard a silky texture. It's an easy dessert to put together for last-minute dinner guests.

cappuccino custard

*NUT FREE   YIELD: 4 SERVINGS

¼ cup plus 1 teaspoon cornstarch

2 cups vanilla soymilk

½ cup turbinado sugar

1 tablespoon instant coffee granules

1 teaspoon almond or vanilla extract

Place the cornstarch in a medium saucepan. Whisk in ¼ cup of the soymilk and cook on medium heat, whisking constantly, for 2 to 4 minutes, until smooth and thickened. Take care that there are no lumps. Do not let the mixture come to a boil.

Whisk in the remaining soymilk and all the other ingredients and continue to cook on medium heat, whisking almost constantly, until the mixture thickens but does not boil, about 10 minutes.

Pour evenly into four 6-ounce ramekins. Cool, cover tightly with plastic wrap, and refrigerate for 4 to 8 hours before serving. Store leftover custard tightly covered in the refrigerator.

You know if you're a peanut butter junkie. I know I am. Peanut butter isn't just for children; it's equally alluring to adults. When I have a peanut butter craving, this tasty mousse is what I turn to.

peanut butter mousse

YIELD: 4 SERVINGS

2 tablespoons cornstarch

½ cup soymilk

1½ cups silken tofu, well drained

½ cup granulated sugar (add 2 tablespoons if using natural peanut butter)

6 tablespoons unsalted creamy peanut butter

1 teaspoon vanilla extract

Place the cornstarch in a medium saucepan. Whisk in ¼ cup of the soymilk and cook on medium heat, whisking constantly, for 2 to 4 minutes, until smooth and thickened. Take care that there are no lumps. Do not let the mixture come to a boil.

Transfer to a food processor or blender and add the remaining ¼ cup of soymilk and all of the sugar, peanut butter, and vanilla extract. Process for 1 minute, stopping to scrape down the sides of the container as needed, until the mixture is completely smooth.

Pour evenly into four 6-ounce ramekins. Cover tightly with plastic wrap and refrigerate for 4 to 8 hours before serving. Store leftover mousse tightly covered in the refrigerator.

Lime complements strawberries magnificently. Perfect for the summer, this light, zesty mousse makes a refreshing finish to any meal.

strawberry mousse

*NUT FREE   YIELD: 6 SERVINGS

1 cup vanilla soymilk

¼ cup cornstarch

2 cups hulled fresh or unthawed frozen strawberries

¾ cup silken tofu, well drained

½ cup granulated sugar

2 teaspoons lime juice

1 teaspoon vanilla extract

Combine the soymilk and cornstarch in a medium saucepan. Cook on medium heat, whisking constantly, for 2 to 4 minutes, until the mixture starts to thicken. Take care that there are no lumps. Do not let the mixture come to a boil.

Transfer to a food processor or blender and add all the remaining ingredients. Process for 1 minute, stopping to scrape down the sides of the container as needed, until the mixture is completely smooth.

Pour evenly into six 6-ounce ramekins. Cover tightly with plastic wrap and refrigerate for 4 to 8 hours before serving. Store leftover mousse tightly covered in the refrigerator.

If you like piña coladas, you'll love this rich, flavorful custard.

piña colada custard

1½ cups silken tofu, well drained

1 cup sweetened cream of coconut, well mixed

1 cup canned pineapple with ¼ cup of the juice

½ cup granulated sugar

¼ cup cornstarch

¼ cup lemon juice

1 teaspoon vanilla extract

Combine all the ingredients in a food processor or blender and process until smooth. Transfer to a medium saucepan and cook on low to medium heat, whisking often, until the mixture starts to thicken, about 5 minutes. Do not let the mixture come to a boil.

Pour evenly into six 6-ounce ramekins. Cool, cover tightly with plastic wrap, and refrigerate for 4 to 8 hours before serving. Store leftover custard tightly covered in the refrigerator.

Tangy and refreshing, orange lovers will find this gel heavenly. Use freshly squeezed orange juice for the very best flavor.

orange 'n' cream gel

¼ cup cornstarch

2 cups soymilk

⅔ cup granulated sugar

¼ cup plus 2 tablespoons orange juice

1½ tablespoons finely grated orange peel

1½ teaspoons orange extract

1 teaspoon vanilla extract

Place the cornstarch in a medium saucepan. Whisk in 1/4 cup of the soymilk and cook on medium heat, whisking constantly, for 2 to 4 minutes, until smooth and thickened. Take care that there are no lumps. Do not let the mixture come to a boil.

Whisk in the remaining soymilk and all of the sugar and continue to cook on medium heat, whisking almost constantly, until the mixture thickens but does not boil, about 7 minutes. Remove from the heat and immediately whisk in the orange juice, orange peel, and extracts.

Pour evenly into four 6-ounce ramekins. Cool, cover tightly with plastic wrap, and refrigerate for 4 to 8 hours before serving. Store leftover gel tightly covered in the refrigerator.

Note: For a beautiful presentation, pour the gel into fancy molds before cooling, loosen it with a knife, and flip it over onto attractive serving plates.

Lemon 'n' Cream Gel: Replace the orange juice with an equal amount of lemon juice, the orange peel with an equal amount of lemon peel, and the orange extract with an equal amount of lemon extract.

Originally known as poor man's pudding, this thirteenth-century British dessert has come a long way. No one would ever guess that you didn't use eggs and dairy cream to make this sensational treat. I challenge you to find someone who doesn't like it. Serve the pudding plain or topped with vanilla soy ice cream or soy whipped cream, sprinkled with cinnamon.

whiskey crème bread pudding

BREAD PUDDING

6 to 7 cups day-old French bread (about 1 loaf), torn into 1-inch cubes

¾ cup silken tofu, well drained

2½ cups vanilla soymilk

½ cup granulated sugar

¼ cup maple syrup

3 tablespoons vegan butter substitute, melted

1 tablespoon vanilla extract

2 teaspoons cornstarch

1 teaspoon ground cinnamon

½ teaspoon salt

¼ teaspoon ground nutmeg

⅓ cup raisins

WHISKEY CRÈME SAUCE

2 tablespoons cornstarch

2 tablespoons water

2 cups vanilla soy creamer, or 2 cups plain soy creamer plus 1 teaspoon vanilla extract

½ cup whiskey

½ cup brown sugar

Variations

- Use dried cherries instead of raisins.
- Substitute rum or amaretto for the whiskey in the sauce.

To make the pudding, preheat the oven to 325 degrees F and oil a 9 x 13-inch baking pan. Spread the bread cubes in the pan. Combine the tofu, soymilk, sugar, maple syrup, vegan butter substitute, vanilla extract, cornstarch, cinnamon, salt, and nutmeg in a food processor or blender and process until smooth. Stir in the raisins. Pour evenly over the bread cubes, making sure they are all coated well. Press the bread cubes gently so they soak up the liquid. Tuck most of the raisins under or between the bread cubes so they stay moist. Let rest for 5 to 10 minutes to allow the bread cubes to soften, occasionally pressing them again so they soak up the liquid. Bake for 35 to 40 minutes, until the top is light golden brown. Let cool in the pan.

To make the sauce, combine the cornstarch and water in a medium saucepan and whisk until there are no lumps. Add the soy creamer, whiskey, and sugar and cook on medium heat, whisking often, until the mixture begins to simmer and thicken slightly, about 12 minutes. Remove from the heat and let cool. Stir prior to serving.

Serve the pudding and sauce warm, cold, or at room temperature. To serve, spoon the sauce over the pudding. Store leftover pudding and sauce tightly covered in the refrigerator.

whiskey crème bread pudding, page 126

vanilla-agave custard, page 128

Ultra-creamy, this custard is just like crème brûlée. If you've never used agave syrup, this custard is a great way to try it out. Agave syrup is derived from the agave plant, found mostly in Mexico but also in parts of the United States, Central America, and South America. It has a relatively low glycemic level and a subtle sweetness; it is the ideal vegan replacement for honey.

vanilla-agave custard

*NUT FREE   YIELD: 4 SERVINGS

CUSTARD

⅓ cup cornstarch

2 cups vanilla soymilk

1 whole vanilla bean
(4 to 5 inches long)

½ cup agave syrup

GARNISH (optional)

⅔ cup mixed berries

Place the cornstarch in a medium saucepan. Whisk in ¼ cup of the soymilk and cook on medium heat, whisking constantly, for 2 to 4 minutes, until smooth and thickened. Take care that there are no lumps. Do not let the mixture come to a boil.

Whisk in the remaining soymilk. Slice the vanilla bean in half lengthwise using a sharp knife. Scrape the beans directly into the saucepan using the tip of a small spoon. Add the agave syrup and continue to cook on medium heat, whisking almost constantly, until the mixture thickens but does not boil, about 7 minutes.

Pour evenly into four 6-ounce ramekins. Cool, cover tightly with plastic wrap, and refrigerate for 4 to 8 hours before serving. Garnish with the berries just before serving, if desired. Store leftover custard tightly covered in the refrigerator.

Vanilla-Agave Crème Brûlée: Sprinkle ½ cup of granulated sugar equally over the filled ramekins. Use a torch to melt the sugar and form a crispy topping.

Notes:

■ Make sure you splurge for a real vanilla bean for this recipe; extract simply will not do if you want fabulous results.

■ Don't throw away the precious vanilla bean pods after you scoop out the tasty insides. Enliven sugar by sticking the opened pods into your sugar jar. Use the flavored sugar in recipes, sprinkle it over grapefruit, or stir it into hot beverages.

■ Look for agave syrup at natural food stores and well-stocked supermarkets, or purchase it from on-line retailers.

Cranberries give this pretty custard some punch. Make it in autumn for a colorful dessert.

pumpkin custard with cran-razz relish

*NUT FREE

YIELD: 6 SERVINGS

PUMPKIN CUSTARD

¼ cup cornstarch

2 cups vanilla soymilk

⅔ cups canned pumpkin

⅔ cup brown sugar

2 teaspoons vanilla extract

1 teaspoon ground cinnamon

1 teaspoon grated orange peel

CRAN-RAZZ RELISH

⅓ cup fresh or unthawed frozen cranberries

2 tablespoons granulated sugar

1 teaspoon grated orange peel

⅓ cup raspberry preserves

GARNISH (optional)

¼ cup chopped toasted walnuts

To make the custard, place the cornstarch in a medium saucepan. Whisk in ¼ cup of the soymilk and cook on medium heat, whisking constantly, for 2 to 4 minutes, until smooth and thickened. Take care that there are no lumps. Do not let the mixture come to a boil.

Add the remaining soymilk and all of the pumpkin, sugar, vanilla extract, cinnamon, and orange peel and continue to cook on medium heat, whisking almost constantly, until the mixture thickens but does not boil, about 10 minutes.

Pour evenly into six 6-ounce ramekins. Cool, cover tightly with plastic wrap, and refrigerate for 4 to 8 hours before serving. Store leftover custard tightly covered in the refrigerator.

To make the relish, combine the cranberries, sugar, and orange peel in a blender or food processor and process just until chunky. Stir in the preserves.

Garnish with the optional walnuts and a dollop of the relish just before serving.

Note: The relish can be made one day in advance and stored in a sealed container in the refrigerator.

Mix and match your favorite puddings, custards, mousses, crèmes, cookies, and toppings to come up with your signature dessert. Be artistic!

pudding parfaits

*CAN BE MADE NUT FREE

YIELD: 6 SERVINGS

PUDDING

1 recipe pudding, custard, or mousse of your choice (see pages 113–119)

MIDDLE LAYER

12 cookies, whole or crumbled, or other filling of your choice

CRÈME

1 recipe crème of your choice (see pages 132–133)

TOPPING (choose one or more)

½ cup lightly toasted sliced or slivered almonds or chopped walnuts, hazelnuts, or pecans

½ cup shredded dried coconut (sweetened or unsweetened), lightly toasted

½ cup sliced fruit or berries

Grated nondairy chocolate

Crumbled cookies

To assemble the parfaits, divide the pudding equally among 6 decorative glass bowls or stemmed goblets. Divide the middle layer equally over the pudding. Spoon the crème equally over the middle layer. Finally, sprinkle the topping(s) of your choice over the crème.

Note: You can make the parfaits with additional layers or with other flavorings or nuts, if desired. If you like, drizzle your favorite fruit sauce, such as Strawberry Sauce (page 93), over the top of each parfait.

Suggested Pudding Parfait Combinations

Pudding or Custard (choose one)	Middle Layer (choose one)	Crème (choose one)	Topping (choose one or more)	Extra Kick (add to any layer)
Almond Pudding (p. 114)	Almond Macaroons (p. 65) Ganache (p. 43) Mocha-Almond Chippers (p. 58) Ultimate Brownies (p. 141)	any	shredded dried coconut (raw or toasted) sliced or slivered almonds (raw or toasted)	dark chocolate-covered espresso beans grated nondairy chocolate
Cappuccino Custard (p. 121)	Almond Macaroons (p. 65) Ganache (p. 43) Mocha-Almond Chippers (p. 58) Pecan Crescents (p. 73)	Cashew Crème (p. 132) Nutty Crème (p. 132)	chopped nuts (raw or toasted)	dark chocolate-covered espresso beans grated nondairy chocolate
Carrot-Ginger Pudding (p. 115)	Almond Cookies (p. 77) Almond Macaroons (p. 65)	any	shredded dried coconut (raw or toasted) sliced or slivered almonds (raw or toasted)	finely chopped candied ginger
Chocolate Mousse (p. 132) Divine Chocolate Pudding (p. 113)	Almond Macaroons (p. 65) Ganache (p. 43) Mocha-Almond Chippers (p. 58) Ultimate Brownies (p. 141)	Cashew Crème (p. 132) Coconut Crème (p. 133) Nutty Crème (p. 132)	chopped nuts (raw or toasted) shredded dried coconut (raw or toasted)	dark chocolate-covered espresso beans grated nondairy chocolate
Mango-Lime Pudding (p. 116) Piña Colada Custard (p. 124) Strawberry Mousse (p. 123)	Almond Macaroons (p. 65) chopped or puréed fruit raspberry or orange preserves	Cashew Crème (p. 132) Lemon Crème (p. 133)	berries citrus slices shredded dried coconut (raw or toasted)	chopped dark sweet cherries Strawberry Sauce (p. 93)
Peanut Butter Mousse (p. 122)	Crunchy Peanut Butter Cookies (p. 71) Ganache (p. 43) Ultimate Brownies (p. 141)	Cashew Crème (p. 132) Nutty Crème (p. 132)	grated nondairy chocolate	heated peanut butter
Pumpkin Custard (p. 129)	Gingerbread Guys (p. 76) Green Speckled Oaties (p. 59) raspberry preserves	any	chopped walnuts (raw or toasted)	pinch each of ground cinnamon, ginger, nutmeg, and sugar raspberries

This is a wonderful topping for any dessert; it also makes a great pudding on its own. Experiment with various extracts and nuts to change the flavor to suit your taste.

nutty crème

YIELD: ABOUT 1½ CUPS

½ cup lightly toasted slivered almonds or raw cashews, or 1½ tablespoons almond butter or other nut butter of choice

1½ cups firm silken tofu, well drained

1 to 1¼ cups powdered sugar

1 teaspoon almond extract

1 teaspoon rum, hazelnut liqueur, amaretto, or liqueur of choice (optional)

Process the nuts into a paste in a food processor, stopping to scrape down the sides of the container as needed. Add the remaining ingredients and process until very smooth and creamy. Cover tightly and refrigerate for 2 to 12 hours before serving. Store leftover crème in a sealed container in the refrigerator.

This crème complements all desserts.

cashew crème

YIELD: ABOUT 1½ CUPS

1 cup raw or unsalted roasted cashews

1½ cups firm silken tofu, well drained

1 cup powdered sugar

1 teaspoon vanilla extract

Process the cashews into a paste in a food processor, stopping to scrape down the sides of the container as needed. Add the remaining ingredients and process until very smooth and creamy. Cover tightly and refrigerate for 2 to 12 hours before serving. Store leftover crème in a sealed container in the refrigerator.

Coconut harmonizes with so many other flavors. This crème captures coconut's essence and will add a special touch to all your favorite desserts.

coconut crème

YIELD: ABOUT 1½ CUPS

1 cup raw or unsalted roasted cashews

1½ cups firm silken tofu, well drained

1 cup powdered sugar (plus 2 tablespoons if using unsweetened coconut)

½ cup shredded dried coconut (sweetened or unsweetened)

1 teaspoon coconut extract

Process the cashews into a paste in a food processor, stopping to scrape down the sides of the container as needed. Add the remaining ingredients and process until smooth and creamy. There will still be some texture from the coconut. Cover tightly and refrigerate for 2 to 12 hours before serving. Store leftover crème in a sealed container in the refrigerator.

This crème is perfect for whenever you want a tangy accompaniment to a dessert.

lemon crème

*NUT FREE

YIELD: ABOUT 1½ CUPS

1½ cups firm silken tofu, well drained

1 cup powdered sugar

2 tablespoons lemon juice

1 tablespoon finely grated lemon peel

1½ teaspoons lemon extract

1 teaspoon vanilla extract

Combine all the ingredients in a food processor or blender and process until very smooth and creamy. Refrigerate for 2 to 12 hours prior to serving. Store leftover crème in a sealed container in the refrigerator.

Luscious TREATS

I often fantasize about desserts, imagining whimsical, colorful concoctions. This section contains all the luscious goodies that can't be classified—a gastronomical miscellany. A huge variety of sweets awaits you in this chapter—your favorites and mine included—from crêpes to gourmet frozen treats, puff-pastry and phyllo-dough specialties, multilayered masterpieces, miniature balls of heaven, cup-sized individual desserts with big flavor, warm and fruity accompaniments to soy ice cream, breakfast treats, gooey bars, fondues, and more, culminating in the most crucial vegan dessert of all: rich, fudgy brownies.

It's almost impossible to mess up a scrumptious treat, so don't be afraid to get creative and put your own twist on a recipe. This chapter offers a range of sweet specialties with a variety of tastes, textures, and temperatures. Enjoy the process, from planning to preparation, as you create your own dessert fantasies.

opposite: coconut tiramisu, page 138

Serve this luscious dessert for the holidays and get ready for your guests to clamor for the leftovers to take home with them. So what if a trifle is British and has its origins in the sixteenth century—in my house, it means holiday time!

holiday pumpkin trifle

YIELD: 18 TO 20 SERVINGS

PUMPKIN CAKE
(makes 4 trifle layers)

2 cups granulated sugar

⅔ cup vegan butter substitute, at room temperature

⅔ cup canned pumpkin

1 cup soymilk

1 tablespoon white vinegar

2 teaspoons vanilla extract

2 teaspoons grated orange peel

1 teaspoon ground cinnamon

4 cups all-purpose flour

2 teaspoons baking powder

1 teaspoon baking soda

PUMPKIN CREAM
(makes 3 trifle layers)

1½ cups silken tofu, well drained

1 cup canned pumpkin

1 cup soy cream cheese

⅔ cup granulated sugar

½ cup turbinado sugar

2 teaspoons ground cinnamon

2 teaspoons vanilla extract

To make the cake, preheat the oven to 350 degrees F and oil and flour two 8-inch springform pans or four 8-inch round cake pans. Combine the sugar and vegan butter substitute in a large bowl and beat with a wooden spoon until creamy. Add the pumpkin and stir until well combined. Stir in the soymilk, vinegar, vanilla extract, orange peel, and cinnamon.

Combine the flour, baking powder, and baking soda in a separate large bowl. Add to the pumpkin mixture and stir until smooth.

Pour evenly into the prepared pans. Bake for about 40 minutes for the springform pans or 28 minutes for the round cake pans, or until the cakes rise and begin to brown slightly and a toothpick inserted in the middle comes out clean. Cool on racks. If using springform pans, slice each cooled cake horizontally with a long knife to make a total of 4 layers.

To make the cream, combine all the ingredients in a food processor or blender and process for about 1 minute, until smooth and creamy, stopping occasionally to scrape down the sides of the container as needed.

To make the custard, place the cornstarch in a medium saucepan. Whisk in ¼ cup of the soymilk and cook on medium heat, whisking con-

Note: Don't be intimidated by the various layers; it really is simple to make and assemble. All the layers can be made a day in advance and assembled two hours before serving. Store the cake covered at room temperature, the cream and custard covered with plastic wrap in the refrigerator, and the topping and relish in covered containers in the refrigerator.

PUMPKIN CUSTARD
(makes 1 trifle layer)

2 tablespoons cornstarch

1 cup soymilk

1/3 cup canned pumpkin

1/3 cup brown sugar

1 teaspoon vanilla extract

1/2 teaspoon ground cinnamon

1/2 teaspoon grated orange peel

CRAN-RAZZ RELISH
(makes 3 trifle layers)

2/3 cup fresh or unthawed frozen cranberries

1/4 cup sugar

2 teaspoons grated orange peel

2/3 cup raspberry preserves

WALNUT TOPPING
(makes 1 trifle layer)

1/3 cup chopped walnuts

2 tablespoons brown sugar

2 tablespoons vegan butter substitute

1/2 teaspoon ground cinnamon

stantly, for 2 to 4 minutes, until smooth and thickened. Take care that there are no lumps. Do not let the mixture come to a boil.

Whisk in the remaining soymilk and all the remaining ingredients and continue to cook on medium heat, whisking almost constantly, until the mixture thickens but does not boil, about 10 minutes. Pour into a large bowl, cover tightly with plastic wrap, and let cool. Then refrigerate for 3 to 6 hours before assembling the trifle.

To make the relish, combine the cranberries, sugar, and orange peel in a blender or food processor and process just until chunky. Stir in the preserves.

To make the topping, combine all the ingredients in a small saucepan and cook on low heat, stirring constantly, for 1 to 2 minutes, until the sugar and vegan butter substitute are melted. Transfer to a small bowl and let cool.

To assemble the trifle, layer the cake and fillings in an 8-inch trifle bowl for a total of 12 layers, starting from the bottom of the trifle bowl to the top as follows:

How to Layer Holiday Pumpkin Trifle

layer 1 (bottom): Pumpkin Cake

layer 2: Pumpkin Cream

layer 3: Pumpkin Cake

layer 4: Cran-Razz Relish

layer 5: Pumpkin Cream

layer 6: Pumpkin Cake

layer 7: Cran-Razz Relish

layer 8: Pumpkin Custard

layer 9: Pumpkin Cake

layer 10: Cran-Razz Relish

layer 11: Pumpkin Cream

layer 12 (top): Walnut Topping

So maybe this isn't exactly a traditional Italian version, but I think you'll like it. Topping it with toasted coconut pulls it all together. Make it in the morning and serve it at dinner for a fancy ending.

coconut tiramisu

*NUT FREE   YIELD: 6 SERVINGS

COCONUT GARNISH

1 cup shredded dried coconut (sweetened or unsweetened; add ¼ cup powdered sugar if using unsweetened)

COCONUT CAKE

1¼ cups all-purpose flour

1 teaspoon baking powder

¼ teaspoon baking soda

1 cup powdered sugar (plus 2 tablespoons if using unsweetened coconut)

¼ cup vegan butter substitute, at room temperature

1 cup minus 2 tablespoons soymilk

1 tablespoon lemon juice

1 tablespoon coconut extract

½ teaspoon vanilla extract

½ teaspoon white vinegar

¼ cup shredded dried coconut (sweetened or unsweetened)

To make the coconut garnish, preheat the oven to 300 degrees F. Arrange the coconut in a thin layer on a baking sheet and toast it in the oven for 8 to 10 minutes, until it just begins to brown slightly. Immediately transfer to a bowl. If the coconut is unsweetened, stir in the powdered sugar. Set aside.

To make the cake, increase the oven temperature to 350 degrees F and oil and flour a 9-inch square baking pan. Combine the flour, baking powder, and baking soda in a large bowl. In a separate large bowl, combine the sugar and vegan butter substitute and beat with an electric mixer until fluffy. Add the soymilk, lemon juice, extracts, and vinegar and stir with a wooden spoon to combine. Add the flour mixture and stir until just combined. Fold in the coconut. Pour into the prepared pan and bake for about 30 minutes, or until a toothpick inserted into the center comes out clean. Cool on a rack for 10 minutes. Do not turn off the oven.

COCONUT CREAM

1½ cups firm silken tofu, well drained

1 cup soy cream cheese

¾ cup granulated sugar

2 teaspoons coconut extract

DIPPING MIXTURE

½ cup hot strong coffee or espresso

2 tablespoons liqueur (such as amaretto, brandy, cognac, Grand Marnier, or rum) or flavored syrup for coffee

1 tablespoon granulated sugar

CHOCOLATE GARNISH

2 ounces bittersweet nondairy chocolate, grated

To make the cream, while the cake is baking, combine all the ingredients in a food processor or blender and process until smooth.

To make the dipping mixture, combine all the ingredients in a small bowl and stir until the sugar dissolves.

After the cake has cooled for 10 minutes, increase the oven temperature to 400 degrees F. Cut the cake in half down the center. Then cut each half widthwise into 5 equal strips, for a total of 10 strips. Turn the strips on their side and arrange them on a dry baking sheet. Toast the strips in the oven for 12 minutes, or until light brown and crisp; do not let the edges darken. Cool on a rack.

To assemble the tiramisu, place a thin layer of the cream in a 9-inch loaf pan. Dip each cake strip in the dipping mixture and lay 5 of the strips widthwise over the cream, so that the bottom of the loaf pan is covered. Spread another layer of cream over the cake strips and sprinkle half of the grated chocolate garnish and half of the coconut garnish over it. Dip the remaining 5 strips of cake into the dipping mixture and lay them widthwise over the toasted coconut. Spread the remaining cream evenly on top. Sprinkle with the remainder of the grated chocolate garnish followed by the remainder of the coconut garnish. Cover tightly with plastic wrap and refrigerate for 4 to 8 hours before serving. Serve cold, in slices.

How to Layer Coconut Tiramisu

layer 1 (bottom): Coconut Cream

layer 2: Coconut Cake

layer 3: Coconut Cream

layer 4: Chocolate Garnish and Coconut Garnish

layer 5: Coconut Cake

layer 6: Coconut Cream

layer 7: Chocolate Garnish and Coconut Garnish

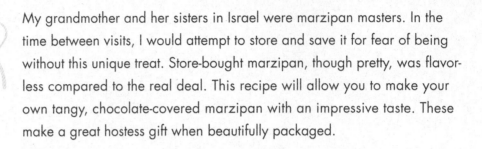

My grandmother and her sisters in Israel were marzipan masters. In the time between visits, I would attempt to store and save it for fear of being without this unique treat. Store-bought marzipan, though pretty, was flavorless compared to the real deal. This recipe will allow you to make your own tangy, chocolate-covered marzipan with an impressive taste. These make a great hostess gift when beautifully packaged.

chocolate-covered almond-tangerine balls

YIELD: 30 BALLS

4 small tangerines

2 cups granulated sugar

1 pound raw or lightly toasted slivered almonds

1 cup nondairy chocolate chips, or 6 ounces semisweet chocolate, melted

Note: Although any vegan chocolate may be used for dipping, rice milk or soymilk chocolate tastes the best.

Squeeze the juice from 1 of the tangerines and strain it through a fine-mesh strainer. Combine the juice with the sugar in a medium saucepan and bring to a boil on medium heat, stirring often. Lower the heat slightly and simmer for 10 minutes. Let cool.

Rinse and peel the remaining tangerines. Place the peels in a small saucepan with enough water to cover them completely and bring to a boil. (Save the fruit to eat at another time.) Boil the peels for 5 minutes (start timing after the water boils). Drain and rinse the peels under cold water. Drain again and pat them dry thoroughly with paper towels so there is minimal moisture on the peels. Remove any black spots.

Combine the peels and the almonds in a food processor and process until finely ground, stopping to scrape down the sides of the container as necessary. You may need to process them in 2 batches, depending on the size of your food processor. Do not let the mixture become a paste. Transfer to a bowl, add the juice mixture, and stir with a wooden spoon until evenly combined.

Shape into 1-inch balls using wet hands. Let the balls rest uncovered at room temperature for 8 to 12 hours to dry out a bit.

Dip the balls in the melted chocolate until evenly coated all over. Arrange the coated balls in a single layer on waxed paper and refrigerate to allow the chocolate to harden. Store layers of balls between waxed paper in a sealed container in the refrigerator.

When it hits you, you know it—that primal need for a sinful amount of the richest chocolate brownies you can get your hands on. It's imperative to have a go-to recipe for gooey, chewy, fudgy brownies, and this one is definitely it.

ultimate brownies

*CAN BE NUT FREE

YIELD: 9 BROWNIES

1 cup all-purpose flour

1/4 teaspoon baking powder

1/4 teaspoon baking soda

2 ounces semisweet chocolate, or 1/3 cup nondairy chocolate chips

3/4 cup granulated sugar

1/3 cup vegan butter substitute

2 tablespoons soymilk

1 3/4 teaspoons vanilla extract

1/2 cup nondairy chocolate chips

1/2 cup chopped walnuts (optional)

Preheat the oven to 325 degrees F and oil a 9-inch square baking pan. Sift the flour, baking powder, and baking soda into a large bowl.

Melt the 2 ounces of semisweet chocolate and all of the sugar and vegan butter substitute in a double boiler over gently simmering water. Alternatively, place them in a microwave-safe bowl and microwave at medium power for 1 minute. Stir. Microwave for 25 seconds longer and stir until smooth. If necessary, microwave for an additional 25 seconds.

Stir the chocolate mixture, the soymilk, and vanilla extract into the flour mixture using a wooden spoon. Fold in 1/4 cup of the chocolate chips and 1/4 cup of the optional walnuts. Spoon and press the mixture evenly into the prepared pan. Sprinkle the remaining chocolate chips and optional walnuts over the top, pressing them in gently so they stick in the batter. Bake for 30 minutes. Cool completely before cutting. Serve within several hours after baking.

Note: To make the brownies easier to remove (and for easier cleanup), first line the baking pan with parchment paper and then oil it.

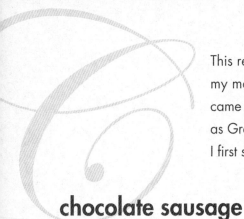

This recipe was a specialty of my grandmother's that was passed down to my mother. It was my favorite indulgence when I was a child. After I became vegan, it was a struggle to create a version that was as moist and rich as Grandma's. I certainly provoked a wave of nostalgia in my family when I first served this easy-to-make version after many years of doing without.

chocolate sausage

½ cup raisins

¼ cup sweet wine, dark rum, liqueur, or water (or a combination of any of these)

1 cup walnut pieces

1 cup nondairy chocolate chips

½ cup vegan butter substitute

⅓ cup corn syrup

1⅓ cup graham cracker pieces (the pieces should be about ¼ to ½ inch)

Soak the raisins in the wine for about 1 hour. Transfer to a blender or food processor and process into a coarse paste. Set aside.

Lightly toast the walnuts in a medium skillet on medium heat. Do not let them brown. Immediately remove from the skillet and set aside.

Melt the chocolate chips, vegan butter substitute, and corn syrup in a double boiler over gently simmering water. Alternatively, place them in a microwave-safe bowl and microwave at medium power for 1 minute. Stir. Microwave for 25 seconds longer and stir until smooth. If necessary, microwave for an additional 25 seconds.

Combine the chocolate mixture, raisin mixture, and walnuts in a large bowl. Add the graham crackers and stir with a wooden spoon until evenly combined. Cover the bowl with plastic wrap and refrigerate for about 1 hour, or until the mixture can be easily molded (not too soft, not too firm).

Cut an 18-inch-long piece of aluminum foil and a piece of waxed paper the same size. Place the foil shiny-side down, then place the waxed paper directly on top of it. Place the chocolate mixture lengthwise in the center of the waxed paper and roll it into a log. Then wrap the log tightly with the waxed paper and foil. Seal, twist the edges, and refrigerate for 4 to 8 hours before serving. To serve, slice the log into thin rounds. Store leftovers in a sealed container in the refrigerator.

Variations

▨ Replace the walnuts with hazelnuts, pecans, or other nut of choice.

▨ Replace the raisins with dried cherries or other dried fruit of choice.

▨ If you prefer the texture of whole raisins, add the soaked raisins and soaking liquid to the mixture without blending.

These decadent treats look more difficult to make than they actually are. Combining chocolate and cherry, creamy and crunchy, all in tiny little packages, yields a marvelous delight.

chocolate-cherry candy cups

*NUT FREE   YIELD: 16 CANDY CUPS

CANDY CUPS

1½ cups nondairy chocolate chips

CHOCOLATE-CHERRY MOUSSE FILLING

¾ cup nondairy chocolate chips

1 cup soy cream cheese

½ cup powdered sugar

2 tablespoons cherry liqueur or rum

1 teaspoon vanilla extract

½ cup fresh or thawed frozen pitted dark sweet cherries

To make the candy cups, line a baking sheet with parchment paper or a silicone pad and have ready 16 mini-muffin cup liners. Melt the chocolate chips in a double boiler over gently simmering water. Alternatively, place them in a microwave-safe bowl and microwave at medium power for 1 minute. Stir. Microwave for 25 seconds longer and stir until smooth. If necessary, microwave for an additional 25 seconds.

Spoon 1½ teaspoons of the melted chocolate into each mini-muffin cup liner. Use a pastry brush or small spoon to coat a thick, even layer of melted chocolate on the inside of each cup. Make sure that the sides of the cups are coated thickly, as these tend to be the most delicate. Place the cups upside down on the prepared baking sheet and allow the chocolate to firm up at room temperature for at least 2 hours. Make sure the chocolate is totally set. Peel the liners off very carefully and set aside.

To make the mousse, melt the chocolate chips in a double boiler over gently simmering water. Alternatively, place them in a microwave-safe bowl and microwave at medium power for 1 minute. Stir. Microwave for 25 seconds longer and stir until smooth. If necessary, microwave for an additional 25 seconds.

Combine the chocolate, soy cream cheese, sugar, liqueur, and vanilla extract in a food processor or blender and process until smooth. Add the cherries and process just until they are coarsely chopped. If you prefer larger pieces of cherries, chop them by hand and stir them into the chocolate mixture. Spoon a heaping tablespoon of the mousse into each of the chocolate cups or pipe it in using a pastry bag. Store the filled cups loosely covered in the refrigerator.

rum balls, page 145

Rum balls are the coveted dessert at the Venetian table. Now you can reproduce these traditional, moist, fudgy treats with this simple recipe. They are truly little balls of heaven!

rum balls

YIELD: ABOUT 48 BALLS

RUM BALLS

½ cup raisins

⅓ cup dark rum

1 cup lightly toasted walnuts or pecans

24 thin vanilla tea biscuits

1 cup nondairy chocolate chips

⅔ cup vegan butter substitute

⅔ cup powdered sugar, sifted

COATING
(choose 1 or a combination)

½ cup powdered sugar, sifted

½ cup shredded dried coconut (sweetened or unsweetened)

½ cup lightly toasted pecans or walnuts, ground in a food processor

1 tablespoon unsweetened cocoa powder sifted with ½ cup powdered sugar

To make the balls, soak the raisins in the rum in a small bowl for 1 to 2 hours. Process the walnuts in a food processor until just finely ground (take care that they do not become a paste). Add the tea biscuits and the soaked raisins and rum to the walnuts in the food processor and process until finely ground. Transfer to a large bowl and set aside.

Melt the chocolate chips and vegan butter substitute in a double boiler over gently simmering water. Alternatively, place them in a microwave-safe bowl and microwave at medium power for 1 minute. Stir. Microwave for 25 seconds longer and stir until smooth. If necessary, microwave for an additional 25 seconds. Add the sugar and stir with a wooden spoon.

Add the chocolate mixture to the raisin mixture and stir with a wooden spoon until well blended. Refrigerate for at least 1 hour, or until the mixture can be easily molded (not too soft, not too firm). Roll into 1-inch balls. Place the coating of your choice on a plate or sheet of waxed paper on a flat surface and roll the balls in it until evenly covered. Store the balls in a sealed container in the refrigerator. For the best flavor, serve at least 24 hours after making.

Espresso Rum Balls: Add 1½ teaspoons instant espresso or coffee granules to the mixture before refrigerating it.

Are you a fudge person? I never thought I was; but I am a chocolate lover and slightly nutty too. Put together chocolate and nut butter and you have a fudge that's easy to make and rich and satisfying. Turn it into "kitchen-sink fudge" by adding all your favorite toppings.

nutty fudge

YIELD: 9 SERVINGS

FUDGE

2 cups nondairy chocolate chips

½ cup vanilla or hazelnut soy creamer

¼ cup unsalted creamy or crunchy nut butter of choice (such as peanut butter, almond butter, or cashew butter)

¼ cup vegan butter substitute

TOPPING (optional)

2 to 4 tablespoons shredded dried coconut (sweetened or unsweetened), **toasted nuts, and/or diced fruit**

Oil an 8-inch square pan. Combine the chocolate chips, soy creamer, nut butter, and vegan butter substitute in a medium saucepan and warm on low to medium heat until melted. Stir with a wooden spoon until smooth. Pour evenly into the prepared pan.

Sprinkle the optional topping of your choice over the fudge and press it in gently so the pieces are lightly embedded. Cool, cover, and refrigerate for 4 to 8 hours. Cut into 9 bars just before serving. Store leftover fudge in a sealed container in the refrigerator.

Chocolate and roses are associated with romance, but they make a heavenly pair themselves. My grandmother used to make jelly from the petals of the roses she grew, and she was willing to go to great lengths to prepare the most complex foods. But these exotic little chocolate balls are really easy to make. Buy rosewater from a Middle Eastern market to add interest and flair to these unusual goodies.

chocolate-rose halvah balls

*NUT FREE   YIELD: ABOUT 18 BALLS

2 cups raw sesame seeds

½ cup nondairy chocolate chips, melted

¼ cup maple or agave syrup

2 tablespoons unsweetened cocoa powder

2 tablespoons rose water

2 teaspoons vanilla extract

¼ cup light toasted sesame seeds

Grind the 2 cups raw sesame seeds in a food processor for several minutes, stopping frequently to scrape down the sides of the container. Once the seeds are ground, continue processing them into a paste. Transfer to a bowl and add the chocolate chips, maple syrup, cocoa powder, rose water, and vanilla extract. Mix with a wooden spoon until well combined.

Using your hands, form the mixture into 1-inch balls. Roll the balls in the ¼ cup toasted sesame seeds and place them in a large container or on trays. Cover tightly and refrigerate the balls for 8 to 24 hours before serving. Store leftover balls in a sealed container in the refrigerator.

Note: For a more robust flavor, use lightly toasted sesame seeds instead of raw. To toast the seeds, preheat the oven to 300 degrees F. Spread the seeds in a thin layer on a baking sheet and toast them in the oven for 6 to 8 minutes. Do not let them brown.

chocolate-rose halvah balls, page 147

spice puffs, page 149

Party puffs are a spicy treat. If you thaw the puff pastry overnight in the refrigerator, you can make these cute and flavorful treats very quickly.

spice puffs

*NUT FREE

YIELD: 21 PUFFS

¼ cup granulated sugar

1 teaspoon ground cinnamon

½ teaspoon ground nutmeg

½ package (8.7 ounces) puff pastry, thawed to room temperature

Preheat the oven to 375 degrees F. Oil 3 baking sheets. Combine the sugar, cinnamon, and nutmeg in a bowl. Divide the puff pastry lengthwise into 3 sections along the creases, according to the way it is folded in the package. Roll out the puff pastry on a flat surface using a floured rolling pin. Turn it over and roll the other side. Cut each section of the puff pastry widthwise into 7 strips, each strip 1 inch wide. Sprinkle a heaping ½ teaspoon of the spice mixture across the length of the strip.

There are three ways to shape the pastry: (1) Fold each strip in half, with the filling in the center, and twist it. (2) Roll up each strip from end to end. (3) Fold each strip into a triangle by folding in a corner, then folding it in again (over itself) in the opposite direction, and continuing the process until you reach the end of the strip. Sprinkle the remaining spice mixture over the top. Bake for 14 to 16 minutes, or until the puffs are a light golden brown and fully puffed. Cool on plates.

I love offering mini-desserts at a party because they are so easy to serve and everyone can sample as they wish, without making a large consumption commitment. Of course, kids adore anything tiny too, so these are always a huge hit with the mini-me crowd. Though fun, these tiny tarts combine the rich, sophisticated flavors of chocolate and raspberry.

fudge-raspberry mini-cups

*NUT FREE   YIELD: 12 CUPS

PASTRY CRUST

½ cup vegan butter substitute, slightly softened but not at room temperature

½ cup soy cream cheese

1 tablespoon granulated sugar

1 cup all-purpose flour

FUDGE FILLING

1 cup nondairy chocolate chips

2 tablespoons vegan butter substitute

¼ cup soymilk

1 teaspoon vanilla extract

GARNISH

¼ cup raspberry preserves

Powdered sugar (optional)

To make the crust, preheat the oven to 350 degrees F and oil a standard 12-cup muffin pan. Combine the vegan butter substitute, soy cream cheese, and sugar in a large bowl and beat with an electric mixer until creamy. Add the flour and knead with your hands until just combined. Do not overwork the dough or it will be tough. Press the dough by heaping tablespoons into each muffin cup, forming a 1/4-inch ridge up the sides. Bake for 8 minutes. Do not turn off the oven.

To make the filling, while the crust is baking, melt the chocolate chips and vegan butter substitute in a double boiler over gently simmering water. Alternatively, place them in a microwave-safe bowl and microwave at medium power for 1 minute. Stir. Microwave for 25 seconds longer and stir until smooth. If necessary, microwave for an additional 25 seconds. Stir in the soymilk and vanilla extract and mix with a wooden spoon until smooth.

Spoon the filling into each cup; it should reach the top. Bake at 350 degrees F for 10 minutes. Remove the pan from the oven and place a scant teaspoon of the raspberry preserves in the center of each cup. Let the cups cool in the pan for about 10 minutes. Using a spoon, carefully remove the cups from the muffin pan. Cool completely on racks. Sift powdered sugar over the cups, if desired. Store the cups in a sealed container in the refrigerator.

Chewy, gooey, sticky, nutty, buttery, flaky, and just plain yummy. Although pralines are traditionally made with pecans, feel free to use walnuts or a mixture of whatever nuts you have in the pantry.

praline bars

YIELD: 9 BARS

PASTRY CRUST

½ cup vegan butter substitute, slightly softened but not at room temperature

½ cup soy cream cheese

1 tablespoon granulated sugar

1 cup all-purpose flour

PRALINE TOPPING

½ cup brown sugar

2 tablespoons maple syrup

1 tablespoon blackstrap or other dark molasses

1 tablespoon vegan butter substitute, at room temperature

¼ teaspoon ground cinnamon

¼ teaspoon salt

1 cup chopped raw or lightly toasted nuts (pecans, walnuts, almonds, and/or hazelnuts)

To make the crust, combine the vegan butter substitute, soy cream cheese, and sugar in a large bowl and beat with an electric mixer until creamy. Add the flour and knead with your hands until just combined. Do not overwork the dough or it will be tough. Cover tightly with plastic wrap and refrigerate for at least 30 minutes or up to 48 hours.

To make the topping, combine the sugar, maple syrup, molasses, vegan butter substitute, cinnamon, and salt in a large bowl and mix with a wooden spoon until smooth. Add the nuts and toss until evenly coated.

Preheat the oven to 350 degrees F and oil a 9-inch square baking pan. Press the crust evenly into the pan, forming a ¼-inch ridge up the sides. Bake for about 25 minutes, or until the dough begins to brown very lightly at the edges. Spread the topping evenly over the dough, leaving a ¼-inch margin at the edges. Bake for about 18 minutes, or until the topping is very bubbly and the edges of the crust are golden. The filling should not be set. Remove the pan from the oven and let cool completely. When cool, cut into 9 squares. Store tightly covered at room temperature or in the refrigerator (for longer storage).

praline bars, page 151

lemon love cups, page 153

Here is another one of my mother's famed specialties. She is known for her melt-in-your-mouth, light and fluffy "lemon love note" bars, which are the inspiration for this recipe. You'll love the startling burst of lemon in the cream and zippy glaze, complemented by the rich crust.

lemon love cups

PASTRY CRUST

½ cup vegan butter substitute, slightly softened but not at room temperature

½ cup soy cream cheese

1 tablespoon granulated sugar

1 tablespoon finely grated lemon peel

1 cup all-purpose flour

LEMON FILLING

¾ cup silken tofu, well drained

½ cup granulated sugar

¼ cup lemon juice

2 tablespoons grated lemon peel

2 tablespoons cornstarch

1 teaspoon lemon extract

LEMON GLAZE

2 tablespoons lemon juice

1½ tablespoons granulated sugar

To make the crust, combine the vegan butter substitute, soy cream cheese, sugar, and lemon peel in a large bowl and beat with an electric mixer until creamy. Add the flour and knead with your hands until just combined. Do not overwork the dough or it will be tough. Cover tightly with plastic wrap and refrigerate for at least 30 minutes or up to 48 hours.

To make the filling, combine all the ingredients in a food processor or blender and process until smooth and fluffy, about 1 minute. The filling can be made up to 24 hours in advance and stored in a sealed container in the refrigerator.

To make the glaze, combine the lemon juice and sugar in a small saucepan and warm on medium-high heat until the mixture bubbles. Alternatively, place the ingredients in a microwave-safe bowl and microwave at medium power for 25 seconds. Stir until the sugar dissolves.

Preheat the oven to 350 degrees F and oil a standard 12-cup muffin pan. Press 1½ tablespoons of the pastry dough firmly and evenly into the bottom each muffin cup, forming a ¼-inch ridge up the sides. Bake for 15 minutes, or until the crust is lightly browned. Cool in the pan for about 10 minutes. Do not turn off the oven.

Spoon 1½ to 2 tablespoons of the filling mixture into each baked cup. Bake at 350 degrees F for about 15 minutes, or until the filling is set. Remove from the oven and let cool in the pan for 10 minutes. Spoon 1 teaspoon of the glaze over each cup. Using a spoon, carefully remove the cups from the muffin pan. Cool completely on racks. Store the cups in a sealed container in the refrigerator.

Note: The glaze provides an extra kick of lemon, but it may be omitted if you prefer. For a fancy touch, place a ripe berry in the center of each cup just before serving.

My husband and I once stayed at a small bed and breakfast in coastal New England where they had the most fantastic homemade granola served with fresh fruit. This is my version of it, although each time I make a huge batch of it, it's slightly different from the time before. Personalize your own granola with your favorite additions.

utopia granola

YIELD: ABOUT 12 CUPS (DEPENDING ON THE NUMBER OF ADDITIONS)

DRY MIXTURE

8 cups rolled oats

1½ cups wheat germ

1½ cups brown sugar

ADDITIONS
(choose as many as you like)

½ cup shredded dried coconut
(sweetened or unsweetened)

½ cup raw slivered or sliced
almonds

½ cup raw pumpkin seeds

½ cup chopped candied
orange or lemon peel

½ cup raw sunflower seeds

½ cup chopped dates

½ cup flaxseeds

½ cup raisins

½ cup chopped raw pecans

½ cup dried fruit
(blueberries, cherries, or
cranberries)

½ cup chopped candied ginger

¼ cup sesame seeds

WET MIXTURE

¾ cup maple syrup

½ cup water

½ cup canola oil

½ cup peanut butter
(salted or unsalted)

1½ tablespoons blackstrap
or other dark molasses

1 teaspoon vanilla extract

1 teaspoon almond extract

Preheat the oven to 200 degrees F and oil 6 baking sheets. Combine the dry mixture with the additions of your choice in a large bowl. Combine the wet ingredients in a small saucepan and warm the mixture on medium heat until melted. Whisk until smooth. Pour into the dry mixture and mix with a wooden spoon until evenly distributed. Spread the mixture evenly on the prepared baking sheets. Bake for 2 hours, or until lightly browned. Transfer to large dishes to cool. Store in sealed containers in the refrigerator.

I have a weakness for huge, fruity, frozen restaurant drinks. So why not have one for dessert? These fantastic adult summer treats are great to serve at a cookout or backyard party or as a refreshing reward after a day of frolicking in the sun. I'll take my drink to go!

frozen strawberry margarita mini-cups

*NUT FREE   YIELD: 15 MINI-CUPS

PRETZEL CRUST

2 ½ cups salted thin pretzels

½ cup vegan butter substitute, at room temperature

STRAWBERRY MARGARITA FILLING

1 pound fresh strawberries, rinsed and hulled, or 1 pound frozen strawberries, partially thawed

1½ cups silken tofu, well drained

½ cup soy cream cheese

⅓ to ½ cup tequila or rum

⅓ cup granulated sugar

2 tablespoons lime juice

1 tablespoon grated lime peel

To make the crust, oil two standard muffin pans. Process the pretzels into fine crumbs in a blender or food processor. Transfer to a large bowl, add the vegan butter substitute, and stir with a wooden spoon until combined. Press into 15 of the muffin cups, using about 1 tablespoon per cup and forming a ½-inch rim.

To make the filling, slice 6 medium strawberries and set aside. Place the remaining strawberries and all of the tofu, soy cream cheese, tequila, sugar, lime juice, and lime peel in a food processor or blender and process until fluffy, about 2 minutes. Stir in the sliced strawberries by hand. Pour evenly into the muffin pans. Freeze the pans several hours before serving. Let thaw for about 10 minutes prior to serving. Store leftovers tightly covered in the freezer.

Frozen Strawberry Margarita Pie: Use a 9-inch pie pan instead of a muffin pan. Slice into wedges to serve.

Note: Silicone muffin cups work well for this recipe.

Impress people with this dessert, which looks much more difficult than it is.
Serve it over Vanilla-Agave Soy Ice Cream (page 157).

banana-caramel swirl

*NUT FREE

YIELD: 4 SERVINGS

¼ cup brown sugar

2 tablespoons vegan butter substitute

3 ripe bananas, sliced in half lengthwise and then once across

1 tablespoon rum, liqueur, or flavored syrup for coffee (optional)

Combine the sugar and vegan butter substitute in an 8-inch nonstick skillet and cook on medium heat until the mixture bubbles. Add the bananas and stir to coat. The mixture will continue to bubble. Turn the bananas over very carefully every 4 to 5 minutes. Cook for 15 to 17 minutes, or until the bananas are lightly caramelized but not completely brown or crunchy. Sprinkle the optional rum over the bananas.

Apple-Caramel Swirl:

Replace the bananas with 2 peeled and sliced apples and increase the brown sugar to ½ cup.

This versatile recipe can be served with all your favorite desserts.

vanilla-agave soy ice cream

*NUT FREE

YIELD: 4 SERVINGS

2 cups plain soymilk

¼ cup agave syrup

1 (4-inch) **vanilla bean**

Place the soymilk and agave syrup in a blender or food processor. Split the vanilla bean in half lengthwise using a sharp knife. Scrape out the beans into the soymilk mixture using the tip of a spoon. Process until smooth.

Freeze in an ice cream maker according to the manufacturer's directions. The agave syrup will separate if it is frozen for a long time, so serve the ice cream immediately after it has frozen or let it thaw a bit and mix it well to recombine the ingredients.

Five-Spice Soy Ice Cream: Add ¼ teaspoon Chinese five-spice powder to the soymilk mixture before processing.

Cinnamon Soy Ice Cream: Add ¼ teaspoon ground cinnamon to the soymilk mixture before processing.

These scones are not too sweet, making them a brunch and breakfast favorite. They also make a handy treat to pack in lunches.

blueberry-lemon scones

*NUT FREE

YIELD: 10 SCONES

BLUEBERRY-LEMON SCONES

½ cup vegan butter substitute, slightly softened but not at room temperature

⅓ cup granulated sugar

⅓ cup soymilk

3 tablespoons lemon juice

1½ tablespoons finely grated lemon peel

1 teaspoon lemon extract

1 teaspoon vanilla extract

2 cups plus 1 tablespoon all-purpose flour

2 teaspoons baking powder

½ teaspoon baking soda

1 cup fresh or unthawed frozen blueberries

LEMON GLAZE

2 tablespoons lemon juice

2 tablespoons granulated sugar

To make the scones, preheat the oven to 350 degrees F and oil a baking sheet. Combine the vegan butter substitute and sugar in a large bowl and beat with an electric mixer. Add the soymilk, lemon juice, lemon peel, and extracts and mix with a wooden spoon. Combine 2 cups of the flour and all of the baking powder and baking soda in a separate large bowl. Add to the soymilk mixture and mix with a wooden spoon to combine. Then knead the mixture with your hands until the all the flour is incorporated. Toss the blueberries with the remaining tablespoon of flour; shake off any excess flour that does not stick. Fold the blueberries very gently into the dough using a wooden spoon or your hands. If the blueberries are getting crushed or you are having trouble incorporating them, just place them aside and gently press them into the scones after they are formed and on the baking sheet.

Form the dough into a 1- to 2-inch-thick disk. Slice the disk into 10 wedges (like a pizza) and arrange the wedges on the prepared baking sheet. Bake for 23 to 25 minutes, or until light brown. Cool on racks.

To make the glaze, combine the lemon juice and sugar in a glass bowl and microwave at medium power for 20 seconds. Stir until the sugar dissolves. Brush the glaze over the scones with a pastry brush just before serving.

Note: Dried blueberries are wonderful in scones and are easier to incorporate into the dough than fresh or frozen blueberries. You can also replace the blueberries with dried cranberries, raisins, or currants. Use ½ to ¾ cup of dried fruit to replace the fresh or frozen blueberries.

blueberry-lemon scones, page 158

fruity chocolate crêpe rollups, page 160

Enjoy these delicious rollups for breakfast or dessert.

fruity chocolate crêpe rollups

*NUT FREE   **YIELD: 4 CRÊPES**

CRÊPE BATTER

1 cup all-purpose flour

⅓ cup granulated sugar

2 ½ tablespoons unsweetened cocoa powder

½ teaspoon baking powder

2 cups vanilla soymilk

8 teaspoons vegan butter substitute

FRUIT FILLING

⅔ cup thinly sliced or diced fruit of choice (banana, berries, mango, papaya, pineapple)

2 tablespoons granulated sugar

1 teaspoon grated lemon peel

½ cup sweetened soy yogurt (any flavor)

¼ to ½ cup raspberry or other fruit preserves

To make the crêpes, sift the flour, sugar, cocoa powder, and baking powder into a large bowl. Gradually add the soymilk, a little at a time, mixing with a whisk or electric mixer until there are no lumps. Do not overmix.

Heat 2 teaspoons of the vegan butter substitute in an 8-inch nonstick crêpe pan or skillet on medium heat. Spoon about one-quarter of the batter into the pan so that it forms a thin layer. If there are any holes in the crêpe, add a little more batter to the pan to cover them. Cook until small bubbles form. Flip the crêpe over and cook the other side for just a few seconds. Remove from the pan and place flat on a large dish. Repeat the process with the remaining batter to make 4 crêpes in all.

To make the filling, sprinkle the fruit with the sugar and lemon peel in a medium bowl. Add the yogurt and stir gently until evenly mixed. Spread 1 to 2 tablespoons of the preserves over each crêpe. Place a scoop of the fruit mixture in the center of each crêpe and spread it lengthwise. Roll up the crêpes and serve immediately.

While traveling in the Czech Republic, my husband's homeland, I met an elderly woman holding a tray of doughy balls that smelled heavenly. I learned through a translator that they were traditional Czech fruit dumplings; but since they were not vegan, I did not indulge. Back in the United States, I figured out how to make this incredible treat without animal products. They can be filled with your choice of fruit and dusted with powdered sugar to taste. Think of them as a steamed doughnut, just not as rich.

steamed fruit dumplings

YIELD: 6 DUMPLINGS

DUMPLING DOUGH

½ cup warm soymilk

2 teaspoons active dry yeast

2 teaspoons sugar

1 cup all-purpose flour

⅛ teaspoon salt

FRUIT FILLING

½ cup canned apricot halves, or 6 pitted canned plums cut in half, drained and patted dry with paper towels

GARNISH

Vegan butter substitute

Ground cinnamon

Powdered sugar

To make the dough, place the soymilk in a small bowl. Add the yeast and sugar, stir, and let rest for 5 minutes.

Combine the flour and salt in a large bowl. Gradually add the yeast mixture, little by little, while stirring. Knead for 1 minute and form into a ball. Place the ball in a clean large bowl and cover it with a clean kitchen towel. Let rest for 40 minutes at room temperature.

To fill the dumplings, roll the dough on a floured flat surface with a floured rolling pin into a 9 x 14-inch rectangle, about ¼ inch thick. Cut it into 6 squares (2 squares across and 3 down). Place 2 apricot halves in the center of each square, fold the dough in and over the fruit, and roll to form balls. Make sure the balls are sealed well. Let the balls rest on the floured surface for 15 to 20 minutes.

Using a large steamer, steam the dumplings over gently simmering water for 20 minutes. Serve the dumplings warm, shortly after they have finished steaming. Garnish with vegan butter substitute, cinnamon, and powdered sugar to taste.

Note: A big bamboo steamer from an Asian market will allow you to steam the dumplings easily.

It's Saturday morning. You don't want cereal again. You don't want frozen waffles either. You deserve something homemade, and these crêpes are just the ticket. You don't even have to feel guilty about serving them! They contain turmeric, which is rich in antioxidants that may help ward off cancer and keep the brain sharp, along with nutritious sesame seeds and whole grains. The sweet-and-tangy orange sauce is the perfect complement.

healthful crêpes with orange-maple syrup

*NUT FREE   YIELD: 4 CRÊPES

ORANGE-MAPLE SYRUP

½ cup maple syrup

2 tablespoons finely grated orange peel

CRÊPE BATTER

1 cup whole wheat flour

¼ cup chickpea flour

1 tablespoon granulated sugar

½ teaspoon baking powder

Pinch of turmeric

1 teaspoon raw sesame seeds

2 cups soymilk

2 teaspoons light olive oil

8 teaspoons vegan butter substitute

Powdered sugar (optional)

To make the syrup, combine maple syrup and orange peel in a small bowl and stir until evenly mixed. Let rest while you prepare the crêpes so the flavors have time to mingle. The syrup may be prepared up to 12 hours in advance.

To make the crêpe batter, sift the flours, sugar, baking powder, and turmeric into a large bowl. Add the sesame seeds. Then add the soymilk and olive oil and mix with an electric mixer or whisk until there are no lumps. Do not overmix. The batter will be thin.

Heat 2 teaspoons of the vegan butter substitute in an 8-inch nonstick crêpe pan or skillet on medium heat. Spoon about one-quarter of the batter into the pan so that it forms a thin layer. If there are any holes in the crêpe, add a little more batter to the pan to cover them. Cook until small bubbles form. Flip the crêpe over and cook the other side for just a few seconds. Remove from the pan and place flat on a large dish. Repeat the process with the remaining batter to make 4 crêpes in all.

To serve, place each crêpe on a plate and fold it in half. Drizzle the syrup over it and sift powdered sugar on top, if desired.

Note: Chickpea flour (also called garbanzo or gram flour) boosts the protein content. You can find it at Indian markets and natural food stores.

healthful crêpes with orange-maple syrup, page 162

Fondue has a unique charm—it's the perfect marriage of entertainment and food. Feature these fondues at your next romantic evening or intimate party. For dipping, serve cubes of your favorite cake or biscuits, skewers of cubed fresh fruit (such as apples, bananas, or pineapples), or whole strawberries.

coconut milk fondue trio

YIELD: 2 SERVINGS PER FONDUE

CHOCOLATE FONDUE (nut free)

¾ cup full-fat coconut milk

¾ cup nondairy chocolate chips

1½ tablespoons turbinado sugar

1½ tablespoons rum, liqueur (such as chocolate, coffee, or hazelnut), **or flavored syrup for coffee** (optional)

1½ teaspoons cornstarch

PEANUT BUTTER FONDUE

¾ cup full-fat coconut milk

2½ tablespoons turbinado sugar

2 tablespoons unsalted creamy peanut butter

1 tablespoon cornstarch

STRAWBERRY FONDUE (nut free)

¾ cup full-fat coconut milk

½ cup fresh or frozen strawberries

2 tablespoons granulated sugar

1 tablespoon cornstarch

1 teaspoon lime juice

To make the Chocolate Fondue, combine all the ingredients in a small saucepan or fondue pot. Cook on low to medium heat, whisking often, until the chocolate melts and the mixture is completely smooth and begins to thicken, 7 to 10 minutes. The mixture should not simmer or boil. Reduce the heat to very low and serve immediately.

To make the Peanut Butter Fondue, combine all the ingredients in a small saucepan or fondue pot. Cook on low to medium heat, whisking often, until the peanut butter melts and the mixture is completely smooth and begins to thicken, 7 to 10 minutes. The mixture should not simmer or boil. Reduce the heat to very low and serve immediately.

To make the Strawberry Fondue, combine the coconut milk, strawberries, sugar, and cornstarch in a blender or food processor and process until very smooth. Transfer to a small saucepan or fondue pot. Cook on low to medium heat, whisking often, until the mixture is completely smooth and begins to thicken, 8 to 10 minutes. The mixture should not simmer or boil. Reduce the heat to very low, stir in the lime juice, and serve immediately.

I am a huge fan of desserts made with phyllo, having Middle Eastern influences from my family and others who wrap all kinds of foods in this special dough. The cigar shape is common in the Middle East, and it is typically filled with spiced meat (I love them prepared with spiced veggie meat) for a savory dish, or ground nuts for dessert. They're similar to baklava, but they are less sticky and more portable, with a subtle yet mesmerizing taste.

nut cigars

YIELD: 12 CIGARS

1 cup walnuts

¼ cup granulated sugar

1 teaspoon ground cinnamon

⅛ teaspoon ground nutmeg

⅛ teaspoon ground ginger

⅛ teaspoon salt

2 tablespoons water

2 tablespoons maple syrup

½ cup vegan butter substitute

½ package (8.7 ounces) phyllo dough, thawed to room temperature (12 sheets)

Preheat the oven to 350 degrees F. Combine the walnuts, sugar, cinnamon, nutmeg, ginger, and salt in a food processor and coarsely grind. The mixture should have some texture but no large pieces. Transfer to a large bowl and stir in the water and maple syrup with a wooden spoon.

Melt the vegan butter substitute in a double boiler over gently simmering water. Alternatively, place it in a microwave-safe bowl and microwave at medium power for 15 seconds.

Unwrap the phyllo dough very carefully. Take 1 sheet and roll it out on a floured flat surface so it is lengthwise in front of you. Use a rolling pizza cutter to cut the sheet in half lengthwise. If you have trouble working with the dough, fold it over lengthwise to double the dough instead of cutting it. Using a pastry brush, spread a very thin layer of the vegan butter substitute over the entire sheet. Place 1 tablespoon of the walnut mixture in a strip about 1 inch from the top of each piece. Roll the dough very tightly from the top all the way to the bottom. Use a little vegan butter substitute to seal the cigar, and then brush some on the outside of the cigar as well. Arrange the cigars on a dry baking sheet. Bake for 13 to 14 minutes, or until they are light golden brown. Cool for 3 minutes on the baking sheet, then transfer to a large plate to cool completely.

Notes

 For ease of preparation, thaw the phyllo dough for 8 to 12 hours in the refrigerator. Then bring it to room temperature prior to preparing.

If you are having trouble separating one phyllo sheet but can grab two easily, you can use two at a time instead of one and follow the same procedure.

It's fascinating how the poppy seed roll is woven into the culinary fabric of so many European countries. It is not surprising, however, since the poppy plant was cultivated in both Europe and Asia for so long. There are depictions of the poppy plant found in Sumerian pictures dating back to 4000 BC. Here is one of the world's most popular cakes made easy by using packaged puff pastry dough.

poppy seed roll

POPPY SEED FILLING

2 cups poppy seeds

1 cup granulated sugar

²/₃ cup plus ½ cup raisins

²/₃ cup vegan butter substitute, at room temperature

½ cup soymilk plus more as needed

1 teaspoon grated lemon peel

½ cup chopped walnuts (optional)

PUFF PASTRY

1 package (17.3 ounces) puff pastry, thawed in the refrigerator for 8 to 48 hours

Small bowl of soymilk

Powdered sugar

Preheat the oven to 350 degrees F. Using a small amount of vegan butter substitute, oil 2 baking sheets and lightly dust them with flour.

To make the filling, grind the poppy seeds in 4 batches in a coffee grinder for about 30 seconds per batch. The seeds should open and release their flavor but not become a paste. Combine the poppy seeds, sugar, ²/₃ cup of the raisins, and all of the vegan butter substitute, soymilk, and lemon peel in a food processor or blender and process for about 1 minute, or until there are no chunks. Stir in the remaining ½ cup of raisins and the optional walnuts.

To make the rolls, divide the dough in half and roll out each half separately on a floured flat surface using a floured rolling pin. Repair any cracks by pinching the dough toward the crack and turning the dough over and repeating the process on the other side so that both sides are sealed. Roll the dough only slightly larger than its original size so that it is approximately 11 x 13 inches.

Note: Make the rolls even faster by using 1 can (12.5 ounces) poppy seed filling. Stir in ½ cup of raisins and ½ cup of chopped walnuts, if desired. Alternatively, make the filling up to 3 days in advance and store it in a sealed container in the refrigerator.

Poppy Seed Jam Roll: Warm ¼ cup of seedless berry preserves or apricot jam and use a pastry brush to spread a thin layer over the dough before you spread the poppy seed filling over it (be sure to leave the 1-inch margin where the soymilk has been brushed).

Using a pastry brush, brush a thin layer of soymilk over a 1-inch margin around the perimeter of the dough. Spread half the filling as evenly as possible (it will be very thick) over each half of the dough, leaving the 1-inch margin with the soymilk exposed.

To form the rolls, work with one at a time. Roll the dough over the filling lengthwise. Pull the dough over the top so that it comes all the way over to the other side and pinch to seal. Bring the edges upward, twist, and seal the sides using a fork to press down on the dough until it is well sealed. When the roll is sealed, flip it over to the other side. Use a fork to lightly prick the roll every few inches but do not puncture it. Repeat this process with the second roll.

Arrange the rolls on the prepared baking sheets. Bake for 40 to 45 minutes, or until each roll is light golden brown. Cool the rolls on the baking sheet for 4 minutes, then carefully transfer them to a large dish. When completely cool, cut off the hard ends and slice each roll into 8 pieces, slicing straight down or diagonally. Dust with powdered sugar.

This is my mother's famous apple strudel, also known by many as "the best strudel I've ever had!" Make sure you have some vanilla soy ice cream on hand to serve with this treat.

apple strudel

*CAN BE NUT FREE

YIELD: 2 STRUDELS, 5 SERVINGS EACH

APPLE FILLING

3 tablespoons raisins

1 tablespoon brandy, rum, sweet red wine, or fruit juice

3 Granny Smith apples (if the apples are very large, use only 2), **peeled**

3 tablespoons granulated sugar

1½ to 2 teaspoons ground cinnamon

1 teaspoon finely grated lemon peel

3 tablespoons chopped walnuts (optional)

PASTRY

⅔ cup vegan butter substitute

½ package (8.7 ounces) phyllo dough, thawed to room temperature (12 sheets)

⅓ cup smooth apricot jam

½ cup plain breadcrumbs

Preheat the oven to 350 degrees F. Using a small amount of vegan butter substitute, oil 2 baking sheets and lightly dust them with flour.

To make the filling, toss the raisins with the brandy in a small bowl. Coarsely shred half the apples and finely chop the other half. Place the apples in a large bowl and add the raisin mixture, sugar, cinnamon, and lemon peel and mix well.

Toast the optional walnuts in a skillet on low to medium heat until they begin to brown. Immediately add them to the apple mixture and stir until evenly combined.

To make the pastry, melt the vegan butter substitute in a double boiler over gently simmering water. Alternatively, place it in a microwave-safe bowl and microwave at medium power for 15 seconds.

Unroll the phyllo dough very carefully. Lay 1 whole sheet widthwise on a floured flat surface. Use a pastry brush to lightly coat the sheet with some of the melted vegan butter substitute. Lightly sprinkle a thin layer of breadcrumbs on top. Repeat with 4 more sheets, laying each on top of the other. Place 1 final sheet on top but do not spread it with the butter substitute or sprinkle it with breadcrumbs. Place the apricot jam in a glass bowl and microwave at medium power for 10 seconds to soften it. Spread the top sheet of phyllo dough with a layer of the jam, using about half of it. Sprinkle breadcrumbs over the jam. Spread half of the apple filling over the breadcrumbs, keeping at least a 2-inch margin around the edges. Fold the left and right edges in, about 2 inches per side. Then roll from the top very tightly to make a thick roll. Gently transfer to 1 of the prepared baking sheets. Repeat the process with the remaining phyllo dough, vegan butter substitute, breadcrumbs, apricot jam, and apple filling.

Bake for 25 to 30 minutes, or until golden brown. Cool on the baking sheets for 4 minutes, then transfer to large plates. Store leftovers tightly covered in the refrigerator.

Notes

▪ For ease of preparation, thaw the phyllo dough for 8 to 12 hours in the refrigerator. Then bring it to room temperature prior to preparing.

▪ If you are having trouble separating one phyllo sheet but can grab two easily, you can use two at a time instead of one and follow the same procedure.

▪ Do not use Panko breadcrumbs, the Japanese variety made without crusts. You can make your own breadcrumbs using stale bread or lightly toasted bread and processing it into fine crumbs in a food processor. Either white or whole wheat bread can be used.

▪ If you wish to double the recipe, the baked and cooled strudels may be wrapped in aluminum foil and frozen. To thaw, preheat the oven to 300 degrees F. Unwrap the frozen strudel, place it on a baking sheet, and bake for 15 to 20 minutes, or until warmed through.

I admit that plain old apple cobbler and apple crisp bore me to tears. If you agree, give this lively, colorful cobbler a shot. Use seasonal fruits to vary your recipe each month, and choose fun cookie cutters to jazz up the dish. Serve the cobbler plain or with soy ice cream or any other creamy topping of your choice.

fruity-berry cookie cobbler

*NUT FREE   YIELD: 10 SERVINGS

FRUIT FILLING

2 cups fresh or frozen berries

2 cups peeled and sliced apples and/or peaches

½ cup granulated sugar

COOKIE TOPPING

½ cup vegan butter substitute, slightly softened but not at room temperature

½ cup granulated sugar

1 teaspoon vanilla extract

1 cup all-purpose flour

½ teaspoon baking powder

¼ teaspoon salt

1 teaspoon ground cinnamon

To make the filling, toss the fruit and sugar in a 9 x 13-inch baking pan. Let rest for about 15 minutes.

To make the topping, combine the vegan butter substitute, sugar, and vanilla extract in a large bowl and beat with a wooden spoon until creamy. Combine the flour, baking powder, and salt in a separate large bowl. Add to the vegan butter mixture and mix well. Knead the dough with your hands to make sure the flour is evenly incorporated. If the dough is soft, cover and refrigerate it for 30 to 60 minutes.

Preheat the oven to 350 degrees F. Roll out the dough on a floured surface with a floured rolling pin to ¼ inch thick. Cut the dough into the shapes of your choice using 2- to 3-inch cookie cutters. Arrange the cutouts evenly over the fruit. Sprinkle with the cinnamon.

Bake the cobbler for 36 to 38 minutes, or until the topping begins to brown lightly. For the best flavor, serve the cobbler warm, within 30 minutes after removing it from the oven. Store leftover cobbler tightly covered in the refrigerator.

Variation: Use up to 1 cup of drained canned fruit or ready-made pie filling in place of the fresh apples and/or peaches. Reduce the sugar to ⅓ cup.

Note: The cookie topping may be made up to 24 hours in advance. Wrap it tightly in plastic wrap and keep it refrigerated until you are ready to roll it out.

ice cream cake, page 172

Just because you don't eat dairy doesn't mean you shouldn't enjoy a fabulous ice cream cake. The following recipes are for chocolate and vanilla cakes; choose your favorite. Alternatively, prepare half of any other cake recipe from this book and bake it in a nine-inch square baking pan; the baking time and other directions will be the same.

ice cream cake

CHOCOLATE CAKE

1¼ cups all-purpose flour

¾ cups granulated sugar

¼ cup unsweetened cocoa powder, sifted

1 teaspoon baking powder

¼ teaspoon baking soda

¼ teaspoon salt

1 cup soymilk

¼ cup canola oil

½ teaspoon white vinegar

½ teaspoon vanilla extract

VANILLA CAKE

1¼ cups all-purpose flour

1 teaspoon baking powder

¼ teaspoon baking soda

½ cup plus 2 tablespoons powdered sugar

¼ cup vegan butter substitute, at room temperature

¾ cup plus 1 tablespoon soymilk

1 tablespoon lemon juice

1½ teaspoons vanilla extract

½ teaspoon white vinegar

To make the chocolate cake, preheat the oven to 350 degrees F. Oil and flour a 9-inch square baking pan. Combine the flour, sugar, cocoa, baking powder, baking soda, and salt in a large bowl. Add the soymilk, oil, vinegar, and vanilla extract and stir until combined. Pour into the prepared baking pan. Bake for about 28 minutes, or until a toothpick inserted into the center comes out clean. Cool on a rack.

    To make the vanilla cake, preheat the oven to 350 degrees F. Oil and flour a 9-inch square baking pan. Combine the flour, baking powder, and baking soda in a large bowl. Combine the sugar and vegan butter substitute in a separate large bowl and beat with an electric mixer until smooth. Add the soymilk, lemon juice, vanilla extract, and vinegar and stir with a wooden spoon to combine. Add the flour mixture and stir until just combined, making sure there are no lumps. Pour into the prepared baking pan and bake for about 25 minutes, or until cake is lightly browned and a toothpick inserted into the center comes out clean. Cool on a rack.

ICE CREAM FILLING

1 pint vanilla soy ice cream or other flavor of choice

1 recipe Ganache (page 43)

TOPPINGS
(choose 1 or more; optional)

Fresh berries (strawberries, blueberries, raspberries)

Chocolate chips

Chocolate sprinkles

Colored sprinkles

Chopped nuts

Shredded dried coconut (sweetened or unsweetened)

Prepare the cake of your choice in a 9-inch square baking pan. While the cake is cooling, line a 9-inch loaf pan with 2 layers of plastic wrap, letting the plastic wrap hang over the edges by several inches. Freeze the pan for 1 hour. About 10 minutes prior to assembling the cake, take the ice cream out of the freezer to let it soften slightly. Cut the cake down the center while it is still in the pan. Then cut each half widthwise into 5 slices.

Arrange half of the cake slices on the bottom of the loaf pan. Spread half of the ice cream over the cake. Then spread half of the ganache evenly over the ice cream. Freeze for 30 minutes. (Put the ice cream back in the freezer for 20 minutes to keep it from melting.) Press another layer of cake gently over the ganache and cover it with the remainder of the ice cream, smoothing it over the cake. Freeze for 30 minutes. Spread the remaining ganache over the ice cream and sprinkle the optional toppings over the ganache. Fold the plastic wrap over the top and freeze the cake for 4 to 12 hours. Carefully remove the cake from the pan and unwrap it before serving. Sprinkle any additional toppings of your choice decoratively over the cake, if desired. Store leftover cake tightly covered in the freezer.

How to Layer Ice Cream Cake

layer 1 (bottom): cake

layer 2: ice cream

layer 3: ganache

layer 4: cake

layer 5: ice cream

layer 6: ganache

layer 7 (top): toppings

ACKNOWLEDGMENTS

Special gratitude to my young sons Kyan and Asher, who are already my expert tasters. If early indications prove correct, I'd say the creative foodie gene was passed along seamlessly. To my mother, who instilled in me a passion for creating innovative and luscious food and provided expert input into this book. And to Milan, without whom this book would not be possible.

This book is dedicated to animals and our earth. I truly hope it will be a source of information that will help inspire people to use fewer animal products and enjoy doing so, too.

Many thanks to the following people who have assisted in the completion of this book: Milan, for his never-ending ideas, unique food styling, creative capturing of the desserts with the lens, and on-target input into the recipes (let this be your credit!). Special thanks to my mother, Gitit, for all her help and inspiration; to my agent Tracy Brown, who believed in *Sweet Utopia* (and me) since the beginning and persevered throughout the many years it took to see this book in print; to my testers, who provided excellent feedback, including Jena, Dianne, Amy, Rae, Rochelle, Genevieve, Kris, and Joanna, my friends, my sister Karen, and props to HG and PD for inspiration. I especially want to thank Cynthia Holzapfel and Jo Stepaniak at Book Publishing Company for their wonderful insight and hard work on *Sweet Utopia*, and the divine book designer John Wincek, as well as the rest of the BPC staff.

ABOUT THE AUTHOR

*Photo by Karen Gordon
(Karenscape)*

Sharon Valencik lives in New Jersey with her husband, Milan (the book's photographer and food stylist), where they are raising their two vibrant, young vegan sons and rescued pets, currently a rabbit and a dog. She comes from a lineage of artistic chef matriarchs and has been baking since age five. Sharon enjoys traveling the world in search of sublime vegan food. Being an avid vegan baker is helping her keep up with her sons' class birthday parties. Please visit www.sweetutopia.com for more information, recipes, and cooking videos, or to ask questions and provide feedback.

ABOUT THE PHOTOGRAPHER AND FOOD STYLIST

Milan Valencik is a fine artist, classically trained musician, and artistic photographer, originally from the Czech Republic. He enjoys cooking, tasting, critiquing, beautifying, and photographing gourmet vegan food. You can see more of Milan's work at www.milanphotography.com.

BOOK PUBLISHING COMPANY

since 1974—books that educate, inspire, and empower

To find your favorite vegetarian and alternative health books online, visit:

www.healthy-eating.com

Lick It!

Cathe Olson

978-1-57067-237-8 $14.95

Simple Treats

Ellen Abraham

978-1-57067-137-1 $14.95

Living in the Raw Desserts

Rose Lee Calabro

978-1-57067-201-9 $16.95

More Great Good Dairy Free Desserts

Fran Costigan

978-1-57067-183-8 $19.95

Raw for Dessert

Jennifer Cornbleet

978-1-57067-183-8 $17.95

Purchase these health titles and cookbooks from your local bookstore or natural food store, or buy them directly from:

Book Publishing Company • P.O. Box 99 • Summertown, TN 38483 • 1-800-695-2241

Please include $3.95 per book for shipping and handling.